How To Draw

SUPERHEROES

How To Draw

Andy Fish

Search Press

This edition published in 2011 by
Search Press Ltd
Wellwood
North Farm Road
Tunbridge Wells
Kent TN2 3DR
www.searchpress.com

A Quintet book
Copyright © Quintet Publishing Limited
All rights reserved.
QTT.HDSH

This book was conceived, designed and produced by
Quintet Publishing Limited, The Old Brewery, 6 Blundell Street,
London N7 9BH, UK

Project Editor: *Martha Burley*
Editorial Assistant: *Holly Willsher*
Designer: *Rehabdesign*
Art Editor: *Jane Laurie*
Art Director: *Michael Charles*
Managing Editor: *Donna Gregory*
Publisher: *Mark Searle*

Printed in China by Midas Printing International Ltd.

Library of Congress Cataloging-in-Publication Data available upon request
ISBN: 978-1-84448-710-3

10 9 8 7 6 5 4 3 2 1

Contents

INTRODUCTION

Superheroes have been around 'officially' since the late 1930s, but way before that they were with us in the form of Greek gods in myths and legends.

Amongst the earliest literary sources are Homer's two epic poems, the *Iliad* and the *Odyssey*. Featuring heroic characters facing unearthly creatures and monumental challenges, these were the fantasy comic book adventures of their time.

Above: Douglas Fairbanks in the *The Mark of Zorro* (1920).

Fictional characters appeared in print – including The Scarlet Pimpernel, Zorro and Tarzan – and although they lacked superpowers, they were idealised versions of physical perfection.

It took comic books to give us true superheroes though, with that strange visitor from another planet, Superman – who was able to bend steel in his bare hands, change the course of mighty rivers and – of course – leap tall buildings in a single bound.

Even the biggest of today's superheroes owes their origins to the heroes of the past. Superman, for example, combined elements from Tarzan (a hero out of his element), Doc Savage (strength beyond that of mortal men) and The Pimpernel (alter ego disguised as a scrawny weakling).

How To Draw Superheroes covers all aspects of creating unique and exciting new superhero characters. The book will give you the guidance and the tools you'll need to create the next great superhero. All it takes is effort from you, the artist.

Above: Superheroes come in all shapes and sizes and this book will help you create your very own, unique creations.

Roots of the superhero

Superheroes were born during the Great Depression of the United States, at a time when the public at large was down on its luck, looking for cheap entertainment – and for heroes to rescue it.

Pulps

Their immediate predecessors were the heroes and antiheroes of pulp magazines. Called 'pulps' because of the cheap newsprint they were printed on and packing more action per dime than ten regular novels today, the pulps featured a dizzying array of characters who fought against the forces of evil: Doc Savage and The Avenger stood for truth and justice whilst The Shadow and The Spider delivered retribution swiftly with their flaming .45 automatics.

Pulp magazines proved so popular that news stands clamoured for similar cheap entertainment and soon comic strips were being collected in reprint editions known as comic books. When they were out of reprints, publishers began looking for new material, and so an industry was born.

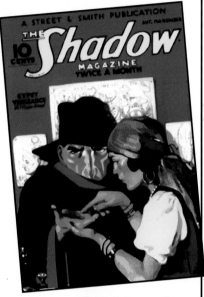

Above: Pulp magazine *The Shadow* was first published in 1930.

Did you know?

Comic books became so popular that eventually pulp characters like The Shadow, Doc Savage and The Avenger were given their own eponymous titles.

The comic industry

Starting with concepts similar to newspaper strips featuring funny talking animals, boy adventures and two-fisted detectives, the new art form of comics did little to distinguish itself from the comic strips – until the late spring of 1938. The writing and art team of Jerry Siegel and Joe Shuster from Cleveland, Ohio, brought a new character to DC Comics (then known as National Comics) after failing to sell the concept to several newspaper syndicates. National liked the character and gave him a cover spot on the first issue of *Action Comics* sending sales rocketing. Superman was born – and with him, a new genre in comic books: the superhero.

Below: The visual inspiration for Superman is clear when you consider the popular entertainment of the time. In his flashy blue hose and bright red cape, Superman would have been equally at home at Beatty Bros. Circus, either on the high-flying trapeze or demonstrating skills of incredible strength.

Changing incarnations

Superman didn't start out being able to change the course of mighty rivers or shift a planet's alignment with the sun. The original version of Superman couldn't even fly – rather he leapt great distances in a single bound, righting the wrongs perpetrated by crooked politicians and vile slum-lords; villains all too familiar to 1938 readers.

Superman's popularity can also be linked to his secret identity, the socially awkward Clark Kent. Readers could easily identify with the bookish Kent, who got tongue-tied around pretty girls. It was a classic power fantasy to imagine themselves able to remove their glasses and turn into Superman.

Identifying with the superhero

Reader identification played a strong part in the success of all the comic characters and whilst a youngster might find it hard to imagine they were a strange alien from another planet sent to Earth in a rocket ship (as Superman was), the following year the groundwork was set for the idea of the regular man honing himself to the peak of physical perfection when The Bat-Man appeared in May 1939. The creation of teenagers Bob Kane and Bill Finger, The Bat-Man owed more to The Shadow than he did Superman, although he too had a secret identity: millionaire Bruce Wayne.

Within a few short years, superheroes were not only conquering comic books, but also radio dramas, the movie screens in the form of animated shorts and motion picture serials.

The superhero was hot and he was here to stay.

Right: During the Marvel Comics revolution of the 1960s, the hero Spider-Man broke the mould by being a teenage hero, rather than being relegated to sidekick because of his tender age.

Typical superheroes

Whether they are able to bend steel with their bare hands, melt guns with their heated breath, live underwater or travel through space, superheroes all share the following traits.

A secret identity

Not only does this give the hero a place for rest, it gives the writer a whole second layer of stories to be able to tell. Would anyone ever guess that Olympic-athlete Larry Busbee is, in reality, the Spybuster?

A story of origin

This sets up the motivation for the superhero's mission (for instance to do good or to fight crime). Some are born from tragedy, others because they were chosen, but the best superheroes have the best stories behind them. Doctor Vampire was motivated to hunt down all manner of supernatural monsters after his family was killed.

A cool costume and a name

Do you think we would still be excited to follow Bob Kane's creation if he had called him Bird-Man like he'd planned if he'd given him a this original costume concept?
In Kane's autobiography, *Batman and Me*, he describes an outfit for his superohero, which originally looked like this.

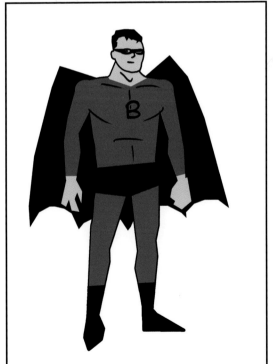

Different superhero characters

Whilst The Bat-Man and The Green Hornet sometimes worked outside the law
– even to the point of being wanted men, there was never any confusion as to
whose side they were on, at least as far as the readers were concerned.

One of the few oddities of the time period was Timely Comics' The Sub-
Mariner – he was a character without clear motivation; in fact some of the time
we weren't even sure he was on our side. He was the first true antihero and he
would eventually lead to the invention of a whole new generation of more
realistic, less purely good characters.

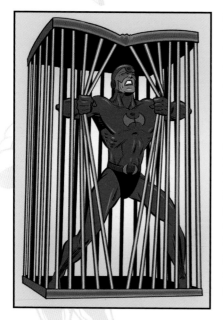

Above: The traditional superhero is often
given a twist with an unlikely weakness or
change of character.

Comic revolution

The revolution took place in
the late 1950s when the characters of
Green Lantern and The Flash were
revived by DC Comics, with more
streamlined costumes and origins
that fit with a science-fiction element.
Whilst the original Green Lantern
owed his powers to the magical
lantern he discovered, the new Green
Lantern encountered a dying alien
pilot who gave him a ring of infinite
power. The new version of The Flash
was given his super speed in a
laboratory accident like his
predecessor, but this time the
explanation given was less vague and
seemed almost plausible.

Above: Presenting superheroes as people with families and relationships helps engender an empathetic reader response.

The Green Lantern and The Flash still behaved a lot like their original counterparts – driven by a sense of duty and service. It wasn't until 1961, when Marvel Comics (previously Timely Comics) began publishing *The Fantastic Four* by Stan Lee and Jack Kirby that the era of realistic superheroes was born. For the first time, superheroes behaved like real people; they struggled with daily life and the difficulties their new superpowers presented. They squabbled with each other like a real family and they faced villains who weren't always purely evil. The comic book world became less black and white – and soon a whole slew of new comic book heroes was born.

This time their collective motivations were very different. Whilst some superheroes still performed with a sense of duty and morality, others did it out of guilt or obligation, often bearing this weight like a cross. Many quit at one time or another, fed up with the weighty expectations of the public and the strain of leading a double life.

Characters like Spider-Man and Daredevil were given their strange powers by scientific accidents – involving radiation. Others, like Thor, were more in the magical camp and still others like The Punisher combined elements of the antihero with the dedication of training oneself to the peak of perfection.

Strange visitors still took on the role of heroes, but now they came not just from under the ocean or from another planet – some came directly from hell and decided to stick around. Whilst they still wore colourful costumes that hid their secret identities, this new breed of superhero had attitude.

Powers and abilities

The ordinary

Some superheroes are ordinary human beings who have trained their bodies to be the best they can be.

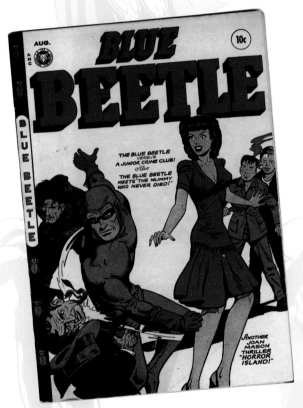

Above: The Blue Beetle was a two fisted brawler who wasn't afraid of throwing himself into the action.

The Black Orchid was secretly Judy Allen, a private investigator partnered with Rocky Ford – who himself was the costumed adventurer Scarlet Nemesis – and neither knew the secret identity of the other. This contrived bit of logic might be the reason they never made it past one appearance in *All New Short Story Comics #2* from Harvey.

Above and right: Judy Allen as her secret identity the Black Orchid.

Daredevil was raised in the Australian outback and mastered the art of the boomerang. When his parents were murdered he devoted his life to fighting crime – and even took a shot at Adolf Hitler in his first issue.

Below: The Marvel Comics version of Daredevil shared only a name with the character from the 1940s who took on the Axis powers during World War II. This new Daredevil was actually a blind man who could see with the aid of radar given to him in an accident involving radioactive waste.

Above: Primarily a hero who battled the Nazis during WWII, The Grim Reaper wasn't above going after an occasional criminal along the way.

The Grim Reaper had a cool spooky costume and left a telltale note signed with skull and crossbones whenever he left a battle scene. He was one of the characters who came along after the introduction of Bat-Man whose motif was of a darker nature than other costumed superheroes. Creatures of the night became dark avengers of justice in the pages of comic books of the 1940s, appealing to those fans whose tastes favoured the anti-hero.

The super powered

Heroes like The Fighting Yank and Captain America embraced the new patriotism sweeping the United States after the attack on Pearl Harbor in 1941. Whilst Captain America gained his powers in a military experiment, The Fighting Yank got his from a magic cloak and hat given to him by the ghost of his great grandfather – who himself was a special agent for George Washington.

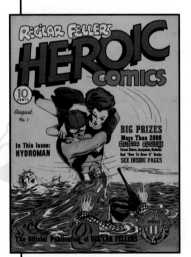

Right: You can't say there isn't enough action on this cover for the French publication *Strange*.

Left: One of the strangest super-powered characters was Hydroman, who had the ability to transform himself into a pool of water.

Right: The Black Terror had a pretty cool costume and got his powers of invulnerability and super-strength from a concoction made out of red ants.

The not super powered but still super strong

Some heroes don't have any clear reason to have super powers but they still manage to perform some super-human feats.

Amazing Man could lift cars and hurl giant boulders with his bare hands, but his origin explained little of how he gained his powers except that he was raised by the Tibetan Council of Seven. He also had the ability to turn into a cloud of green vapour, just in case hurling cars wasn't enough.

Above: Amazing Man.

Left: Sheena was pretty much a female Tarzan – her greatest powers included being able to live alone in the jungle, talk to animals and walk around the rough terrain without shoes on.

Above: Cat-Man and his sidekick, The Kitten.

Cat-Man wasn't a complete rip-off of Bat-Man, at least not once you got past his cape, pointy eared cowl and sidekick. Cat-Man was raised in the jungles of Burma by a Tigress when the rest of his family were killed by bandits. Over the years he gained all the powers of the cat family including the ability to see in the dark, leap incredible lengths and climb virtually anything – as an adult he decided to return to America to fight crime.

His greatest power was the ability to come back to life – i.e. a cat's nine lives. His sidekick, The Kitten, was the first and one of the only female sidekicks in comic history.

Right: Sidekicks were first introduced around 1940 with the appearance of Robin the Boy Wonder as Batman's right hand man – but heroes have had sidekicks seemingly forever in literature – just ask Dr Watson about his work with Sherlock Holmes.

The armoured hero

Armoured superheroes go back much further than Iron Man. Bozo the Robot (sometimes called Bozo the Iron Man) was a robot created for evil purposes by the nefarious Dr Von Thorp, who planned to use the robot to conquer the world. Luckily for us, Thorp's plan was overheard by Hugh Hazzard who took him out and commandeered the robot for the benefit of mankind.

At times Bozo was sent off by remote control and at others Hugh Hazzard was actually inside the suit handling the controls. Either way, he ushered in a new era of scientific crime fighting – the hero in a powerful suit. This idea appealed to readers who could identify with an ordinary person attaining super powers through the use of scientific invention.

Above: The antihero Bozo the Robot in *Smash Comics*, published in 1949.

The superheroines

Superheroines started out as part of a male hero franchise. Mary Marvel was Captain Marvel's little sister but soon became almost as popular to readers as her big brother was.

Eventually superheroines came into their own – Wonder Woman owed her origin to no man and others could make the same claim.

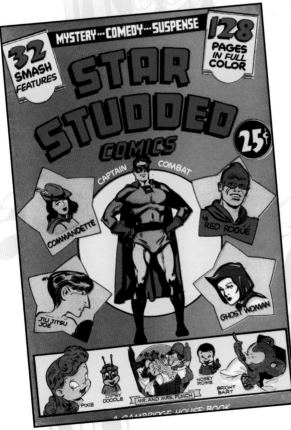

Left: Ghost Woman and The Commandette were often the cover stars of star-studded comics in the mid-1940s.

Ghost Woman gained her powers on a lonely country road after she was killed in a car accident. At the same time she gained the ability to interact with supernatural creatures who roam the earth. Her first encounter was to save her friend John from a Werewolf attack – after which he vowed to fight the supernatural with Ghost Woman at his side.

The Commandette was actress and stunt woman Betty Babble who adopted the role for her latest film, but took it on in real life when she had to track down a criminal who had framed a friend for murder. She used her considerable skill as both a stunt woman and judo expert to aid her in her fight against crime.

Above: Rulah the Jungle Goddess.

Rulah the Jungle Goddess gave Sheena a run for her money – a rich orphan whose plane crashed in the African Jungle, she had a knack for making bikinis from the skin of giraffes. Rulah was not only an expert at jungle life and survival in such a tough environment, she also gained the knowledge of 'jungle magic' which aided her whenever her writers felt they had written themselves into a corner and needed something extra to help her out.

Lightning Girl was pretty tough, often pushing her way to the front of a fight. After a villain's attempt to kill her with electricity backfires, she ends up gaining the same powers as Lightning Man and soon the two team up.

Many superheroines seemed to have been created for the sole reason of providing a victim for the heroes to save, as this cover of *Wonder Comics #11* seems to show – Wonder Man (who had a rocky career due to his similarities to DC Comics' Superman) fights a alien intent on no good whilst Wonder Girl does her best not to faint.

Left: Wonder Girl spent most of her career being captured by villains or forgetting her cosmic belt and being left behind.

Left: Jill Trent, Science Sleuth, was more than a match for any villain and she didn't need a man to help out. With the aid of her best friend, Daisy Smythe, the two travelled the world, quite capable of handling themselves in a fight.

Regardless of how they got their powers, superheroines all had similar motivations in carrying out their mission for the common good. Some did it because of a sense of duty, whilst others did it for justice.

Chapter 1

Tools, techniques and basic skills

TAKING YOU THROUGH THE BASIC ELEMENTS OF CREATING REALISTIC CHARACTERS AND BACKGROUNDS, THIS CHAPTER IS A FANTASTIC STARTING POINT FOR YOUR WORK.

YOUR STUDIO

You don't need a formal studio to create your superheroes, but an ideal situation would be to have a designated area that you can go to when you are working. Whether it's a spare room or a corner of the kitchen, there are a few things you can do to help ensure success.

A drafting table and chair with a good lamp is your best option, but not everyone has them and that shouldn't stop you.

A standard table can work, but if you are working on a flat table, get yourself a board or an easel that you can rest on your lap so that your work faces you at about a 45° angle – this will prevent your work from appearing distorted.

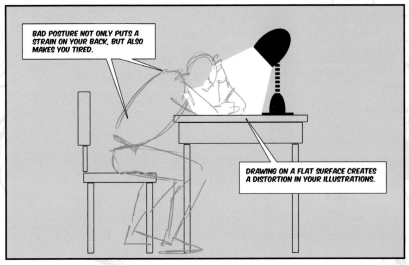

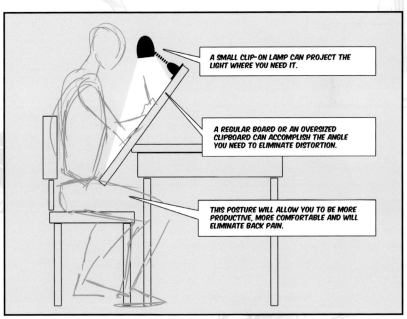

TRADITIONAL TOOLS

Although digital methods are increasingly popular in this field of illustration, a good working knowledge of traditional methods and the right tools is vital.

Pencils

Higher-quality pencil makers glue the lead throughout the pencil so breakage from rough handling isn't an issue.

SOFTEST LEAD

9H 8H 7H 6H 5H 4H 3H 2H H F B 2B 3B 4B 5B 6B 7B 8B 9B

HARDEST LEAD   <<<<<<<<<<<<<<<<<<<<<   >>>>>>>>>>>>>>>>>>>>>

Above: Pencils are graded based on the hardness or softness of the lead.

When grading pencils, 'H' stands for hard whilst 'B' stands for black – a softer lead produces a darker (blacker) line. A hard lead produces a lighter line.

Left: Mechanical pencils never require sharpening and can be fitted with any grade of lead.

Coloured pencils

There is a lot of choice when it comes to coloured pencils – it's worth trying out two or three different brands to see which one produces the colour you like. The better brands of coloured pencil actually glue the lead inside the pencil so it won't shatter with everyday handling. A good way to test a pencil is to hold the pencil up to your ear and shake it – if you hear or feel something loose it's a pretty good bet the lead is broken inside the wood and it'll just fall out when you sharpen it.

Erasers

The soft white erasers are the best way to go – they erase completely and cleanly.

Above: A white eraser can avoid smudging or blots of pencil, but a kneaded eraser is also popular with artists as it can be washed, so it lasts for a longer time.

Left: A quill is an inking tool that is dipped into a bottle of ink and then used to put a line down on the paper. Quills come in a variety of sizes and point shapes.

Far left: Waterproof black India ink comes in a variety of bottle sizes.

Pen and ink

Disposable pens work fine, but they don't give a great line. Microns and Sharpies might be easy to use but if you choose a good brush or a nice titanium quill with some high-quality ink you'll be amazed at the difference – and it's how the pros work.

Waterproof ink is a more permanent kind of ink and usually gives a richer, fuller overall black. It is a more archival type of ink than a water-based ink. Pigment ink is thicker and can take quite a while to dry. The ink sits on top of the paper it's applied to rather than becoming absorbed like other inks.

The application of ink to illustrations can be handled with a variety of tools.

Brushes

A good brush is one the artist can control when putting down an ink line. It's up to the individual artist to find a brush they feel comfortable working with. Page 35 shows the effects created by using a no. 2 small round brush.

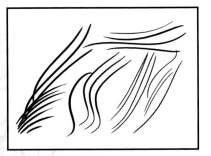

Left: The best way to get a good, smooth ink line with a brush is to hold the brush in a comfortable manner and keep your wrist straight – pull the bristles towards you as you work. With a little practice you'll soon be a master.

Types of hatching

1 Hatching: Use single lines that run parallel to each other – sometimes varying the spacing.

2 Cross-hatching: Simply take hatching and cross it with another set of hatched lines.

3 Free-hatching: A somewhat less formal and more energetic method of cross-hatching. Begin with a series of hatched lines and then cross them with lines that are very loose – essentially scribbles.

4 Patch-hatching: An almost quilt-like quality of filling in a large area with similarly patterned hatched areas. It's effective in larger areas of an illustration.

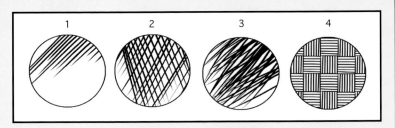

Right: Many good art supply shops will have samples of their paper offerings that you can draw on.

Left: Bristol is a form of paper or board popular with illustrators. It comes in different plies, from 1 ply (very thin) to about 5 ply (very thick). The surface of the Bristol is offered as either 'smooth' or 'vellum' (which has something of a toothy texture).

Paper and Bristol

There are more kinds of paper than there are stars in the heavens or at least that's what Shakespeare might have told us if he ran a craft shop.
Paper is judged on its thickness (ply), texture and how it reacts to various art supplies.

Sketchbook

A sketchbook is an important tool as well – it doesn't have to be an expensive one, but it should be one that you enjoy drawing in every day. It shouldn't just be used for drawing the stuff you like to draw. Rather you should challenge yourself to draw things you don't like – street lights, traffic signals, different sized and shaped people. Take it with you each day and draw from observation. You'll be amazed at how fast you'll improve if you keep at it.

Computer and scanner

Mac or PC doesn't matter much anymore – just get the most powerful machine and the best-quality scanner you can afford. They'll pay for themselves in timesaving.

It's always good to get as much RAM memory as you can afford. Developers are constantly upgrading their software, which usually means more RAM is required of the latest version. It will also help if you choose to run more than one painting application at once.

A digital tablet such as a 30 x 23 cm (9 x 12 in) Wacom tablet is recommended if you are to start working on your art regularly. A large tablet enables you to use broader strokes with arm movements rather than just small hand and wrist movements.

TIP
Try wrapping a piece of paper around your digital tablet to give it a more natural feel when you're drawing on it. Tape it down on the back of the tablet or off of the screen. Never put tape on the screen itself.

Above: A good monitor at a large size 60 cm (24 in) is beneficial to visual artists. This is important because it is easier to work into large portions of the painting without always having to zoom in.

BASIC TECHNIQUES

Creating likeness in a character is difficult without a basis in facial proportions – you may find the eyes have a habit of being too close together or the nose looks out of proportion. The following steps will help you achieve realism.

The basic head

Step 1: Draw a vertical line down the centre of the head. Make sure you keep the features balanced. This'll help you when you do a three-quarter view, as well (see example below). Now draw a horizontal line at the centre point for the eye line.

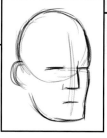

Left: Using proportional lines helps us when we draw the head at a ½ angle too.

Step 2: Halfway from the tip of the chin to the eye line is the nose line. Draw a small horizontal line there. Halfway from the nose to the chin is where the mouth goes. Draw a slightly wider horizontal line there.

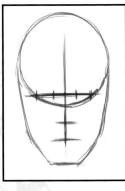

Step 3: On the eye line, mark off division lines for the eye sockets. The space between the eyes is the same size as the eyes themselves. Draw these four lines to create space for the eyes.

Step 4: Start working in the details of the eyes beginning with the upper eyelid – this line should be slightly heavier to indicate shadow.

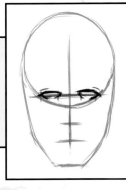

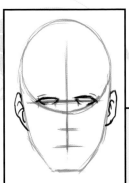

Step 5: Sketch in the details for the ears – keeping them simple is important.

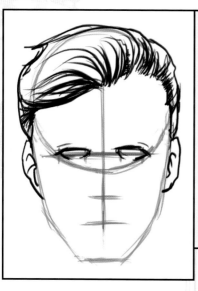

Step 6: Hair adds a lot of character to your, er, character! It's a good idea to keep a small sketchbook with you so that when you see someone with a really great (or unique) hairstyle you can make a quick note of it so you can use it later. Build the hair up from the root lines. Leaving the crown of the head with less lines will make the hair look shiny and clean.

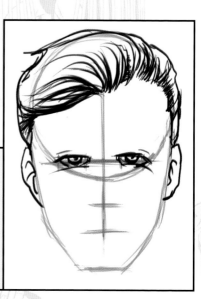

Step 7: Start the eyes with simple three-quarter circles placed slightly up under the lid. Having the eyes sitting under the lids makes them appear more natural.

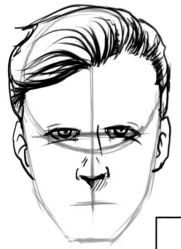

Step 8: Work in the nose – using the basic shape of a V and building the area around the nostrils. Then indicate the bridge of the nose on one side.

Step 9: Add eyebrows – they should be thicker in the centre of the head and get thinner as they taper out. Finally, add a mouth using a simple flattened M shape indicating the shape of the lip with a line both underneath and above the chin.

Basic human proportions

It's important to understand proportions when trying to depict the human figure.

Take this illustration of the human figure by Leonardo Da Vinci (slightly tweaked):

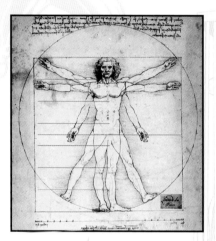

The red lines measure the figure's height – as you can see, a normal-sized person is six to seven heads tall, whilst the centre of the figure is at crotch level, as indicated by the blue line. When the hands are at the figure's side you can see that the wrists fall to around the middle line of the figure and the fingers extend down to the first third of the thigh.

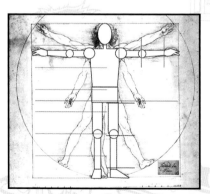

If you break the figure down into raw shapes you can see that the upper arm and the forearm are roughly the same length as shown by the green lines, whilst the upper leg and the lower leg are also about the same length as indicated by the purple lines.

Using these basic shapes to make new figures you can then do virtually any pose and create an amazing array of action positions.

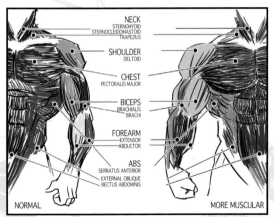

Comparing the structure of a muscular figure with a muscle bound figure helps us understand how these muscles exaggerate and expand and they grow bigger, but still follow the basic rules and shapes of anatomy.

You also need a pretty good understanding of anatomy and the placement of muscles if you want your superhero to look 'right'.

We can see from the illustration above that the figure on the left is very muscular, but not muscle-bound. Note especially the biceps, forearms and shoulder muscles of both figures. You can see, as the muscled figure is bulked up, how the mass of these muscle groups is increased.

How to draw hands

Learning to draw hands is one of the most important things an artist can master. Remember you can always look at your other hand for reference – the traditional way to draw a hand is pretty straightforward.

Step 1: Start with a basic square shape, with very slightly bent sides.

Step 2: If you look at your non-drawing hand you can see the way your fingers come off the base of your hand. The index finger and the pinky are at either end of the square, coming off the very edges on both sides. In the bottom right-hand (or left-hand) corner is where the thumb branches off.

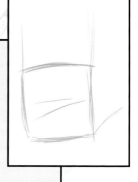

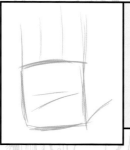

Step 3: Draw in the middle finger and the ring finger – equally spaced between the already-drawn index finger and pinky. Note, by looking at your own hand, the relative lengths of each finger.

Step 4: Go around the outlines you've drawn, adding a layer of flesh onto the hand. Note that the tips of each finger are somewhat rounded and the thumb tip is slightly squared off.

Step 5: Tighten the lines up around the hand and indicate the bend lines of your palm, again using your other hand as reference to see where these lines are.

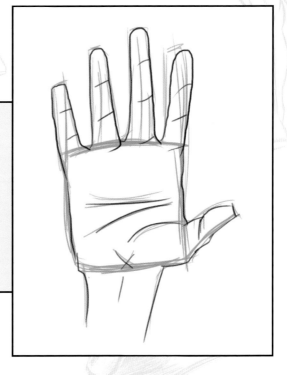

Drawing evil hands

Nothing says evil like a pair of bony hands – the evil hand take a bit more imagination, because you can't use your other hand for reference, but you can use it as a base to build on.

Step 1: Start with the same square-type shape as you did for the regular hand – only this time the emphasis will be on the length of the fingers and the bony knuckles.

Step 2: Work in some of the details that will make the hand evil-looking. Using your own hand as reference again, you can see how the fingers and the knuckles are connected. Stretch the length of the fingers a bit and bulge up the knuckles a bit more.

Step 3: Now start going over the prep lines with ink and a brush. Follow the base already put down.

Step 4: The lines and texture on the top of the hands will add to the sense that these hands belong to a villain. They don't use a lot of moisturiser in lairs, so the hand should appear weathered and worn.

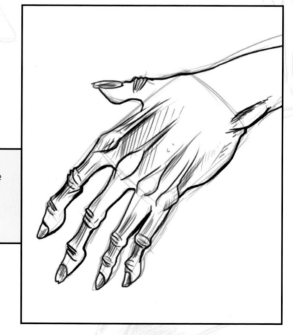

Step 5: Finish off the hand, adding a few bumps and hairs.

Composition

This comprises the elements in your illustration. Creating good composition isn't hard, but it does require practice and thought.

Let's take a quick sketch of a superhero standing in front of a generic looking building – we want to concentrate on the composition rather than the drawing.

It's good to have some background to establish where the character exists rather than just a blank white space. Notice, however, how the figure sits squarely inside the dimension of the building, to the point that his right leg sits along the edge of the building. Even though this could certainly happen in real life, as you design your composition you need to take things like this into account.

By shifting the building a few degrees over we move it off that right knee which gives a better composition, but it's still lacking balance. One technique that can help when trying to improve composition is to divide the illustration into quarters.

The figure sits dead centre in the illustration – that's not always a bad thing but it can make a composition look stiff. Increasing the elements in the background fills the empty areas. Note that each building has been placed so that the buildings are overlapping and getting darker as they go into the background.

As mentioned above, sometimes not centering the main figure makes for a better composition – and sometimes less is better so try cropping the image.

When the image is quartered, the figure sits off-centre – the background still has effective elements and each of the quarters has something of interest in it, making it stronger overall.

Movement

To make the character come alive you need to give it some movement. If you simply pose a figure straight it looks unnatural.

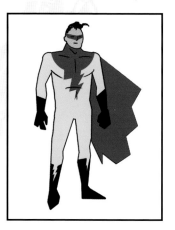

Superhero in action

Whilst it's a good idea to use a stagnant figure to work out the details and colour scheme of your character, this should be used only whilst you are working out your costume design. To show off the dynamics of the character, impose movement and action on the figure.

TIP

Keeping a figure in motion makes the illustration more dynamic – look at this first example. It's a perfectly good drawing, but his overall stance makes it seem like he's waiting for someone to snap his picture.

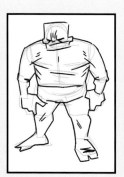

With this second take, the figure's form looks more like we snapped a picture whilst he was in motion – which creates a much more interesting stance.

Once you've worked out your character's costume details and colouring, put him in motion, like you've captured him in the middle of some action, which will make your character much more dynamic looking.

Perspective

You'll need a good ruler for this exercise.

Have you ever stood at the end of a road and noticed that it looks as if the two sides connect at the horizon? That's perspective.

Perspective is a mathematical system of rendering 3D objects on a 2D surface (the paper).

Step 1: Start with a horizon line – a straight line that goes across the page. The horizon line is the eye line of the reader. If you were to stand outside in a wide-open area the line at which the ground intersects with the sky would be the horizon line.

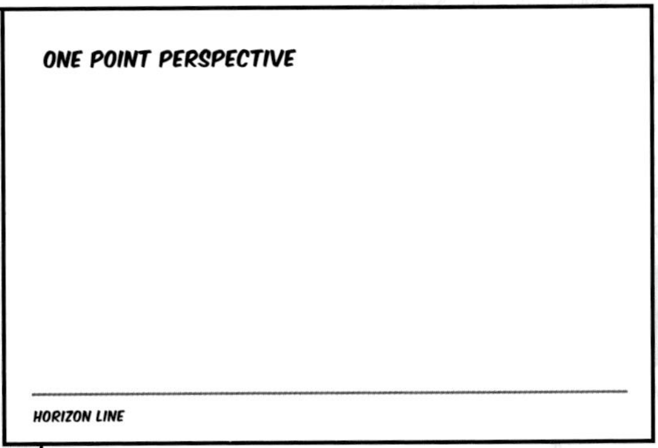

ONE POINT PERSPECTIVE

HORIZON LINE

ONE POINT PERSPECTIVE

HORIZON LINE

VANISHING POINT

Step 2: Now set a vanishing point (VP) on the horizon line. Note that it's important to use an X to mark the VP because that point needs to be precise. A dot might accidentally grow as you work on the drawing.

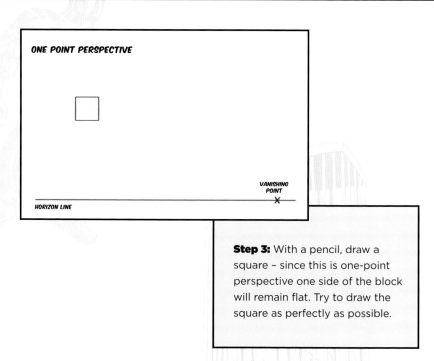

ONE POINT PERSPECTIVE

VANISHING
POINT

HORIZON LINE

Step 3: With a pencil, draw a square – since this is one-point perspective one side of the block will remain flat. Try to draw the square as perfectly as possible.

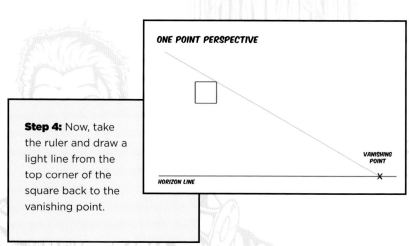

ONE POINT PERSPECTIVE

VANISHING
POINT

HORIZON LINE

Step 4: Now, take the ruler and draw a light line from the top corner of the square back to the vanishing point.

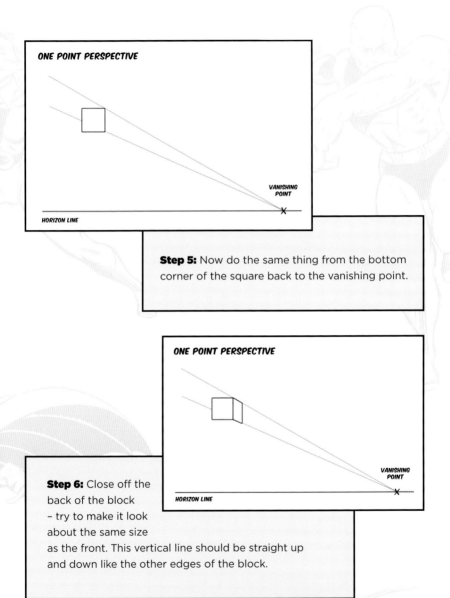

ONE POINT PERSPECTIVE

VANISHING POINT

HORIZON LINE

Step 5: Now do the same thing from the bottom corner of the square back to the vanishing point.

ONE POINT PERSPECTIVE

VANISHING POINT

HORIZON LINE

Step 6: Close off the back of the block – try to make it look about the same size as the front. This vertical line should be straight up and down like the other edges of the block.

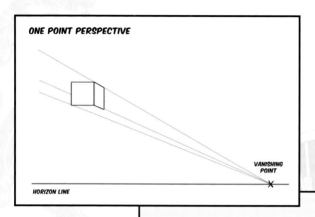

Step 7: Take a pencil and draw a line from the bottom left corner of the block back to the vanishing point.

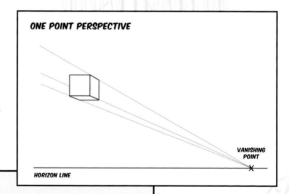

Step 8: All that's left is to close off the bottom line of the block – and that horizontal line goes straight across.

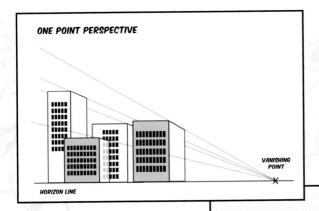

ONE POINT PERSPECTIVE

VANISHING POINT

HORIZON LINE

Step 9: By repeating the steps above, you can create a cityscape out of blocks.

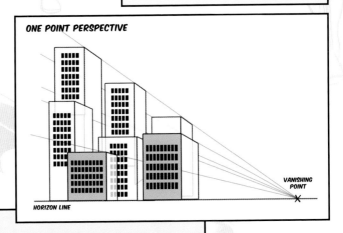

ONE POINT PERSPECTIVE

VANISHING POINT

HORIZON LINE

Step 10: You can even stack the blocks on top of each other to build up skyscrapers.

Tone

Tone is the effect of adding grey to black-and-white artwork, which enhances it by emphasising form, mood or shadow.

There are several methods for creating tone:

- Using sheets of mechanical tone available at most art supply shops.

- Using the grey wash water created by dipping a paintbrush into a small cup of water mixed with a very small amount of ink.

- Applying it using a computer program (such as Photoshop).

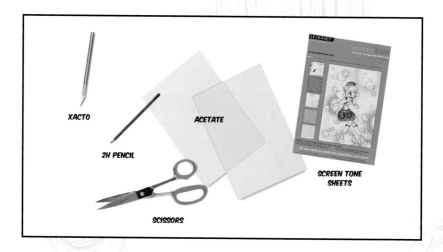

XACTO

2H PENCIL

ACETATE

SCISSORS

SCREEN TONE
SHEETS

Applying mechanical tone by hand involves laying the sheet over the artwork and then cutting out the areas you don't want covered using a very sharp Xacto Knife.

Above: Applying tone from commercial sheets involves placing it onto your image and then cutting away the parts you don't want. Practice to achieve a pressure with the Xacto blade so you don't cut the paper.

Above: See the difference? Nicely placed tone can give the work a polished look and it also gives a sense of form, keeping it from looking too flat.

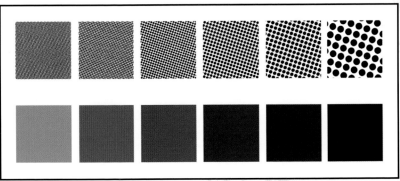

Above: The degree of grey achieved is based on the percentages of blacks and whites. These tones are sometimes made out of a series of screened dots, with the amount of space between them determining the value of the grey colour.

Keep in mind that when printing it is normal for greys to appear slightly darker (usually 10%) than what you might see looking at the original art – therefore you should always fall back 10% in setting the value. (Translation: If you want the printed art to appear with a 40% tone you should apply a 30% tone to the page.) Note too that anything above 80% might as well just be black, since you probably won't see any difference when it's printed.

Left: Tone effects can also be added by hand using wash, which is watered down or thinned black ink.

TIP

Adding tone with a brush involves a bit of practice. Mix your wash in a clean small bottle. Rinse your brush off so it's clean and fairly dry – then dip it in the ink wash and you'll get a smooth shade.

Using a computer to apply tone

Welcome to the twenty-first century. Most artists now use Photoshop or similar software to apply grey tones to their art – it's clean, works great and completely eliminates the chances for error since everything done can be undone. Plus it's about a million times faster.

Step 1: Scan the artwork into the chosen computer program at 300 dpi as a greyscale image. Here, Photoshop has been used.

Step 2: In Photoshop you can add a layer over the artwork and then fill that layer with a grey colour using the Paint Bucket tool. Make sure your grey layer is set to multiply so you can see the image through the colour.

Step 3: Go to Filter>
Sketch>Halftone pattern
and see what you can
achieve when you
experiment with the
settings. You can also go
to Filter>Pattern maker
and do much the same
thing. (Some artists even
scan in sheets of tone and
then use cut and paste to
add it to their pages.)

Step 4: Now using either a
graphics tablet and the Eraser
tool or the Polygonal Lasso tool
in Photoshop, you can remove
all the grey parts you don't want
– and soon you'll have an
effectively toned page.

Tone effects

Experiment – you'll be surprised at the number of effects you can achieve.

Step 1: Start with a line drawing of a face. It's a perfectly good line drawing but it has a kind of colouring-book feel to it.

Step 2: Adding blacks to the hair and a grey tone to the background, as well as a bit of shading on the face, enhances the image.

Step 3: Adding a shadow to the front of the face adds an air of mystery. This would indicate that the face is being lit from behind.

Step 4: A strong shadow on one side of the face gives a sense of offside lighting and creates a different mood.

Step 5: If you put a strong light directly above the face, you can create a heavier shadow in the eye sockets, under the nose and under the chin – giving the character a sense of menace.

Step 6: Setting the light from below instead gives the effect of discovery or higher power.

Colour

Hues and tones of colour can affect the mood and vibrance of a piece of work.
Learning to work with colour is a key skill you can take forwards into your art.

Complementary colours

Complementary colours are opposite each other on the colour wheel and
intensify each other.

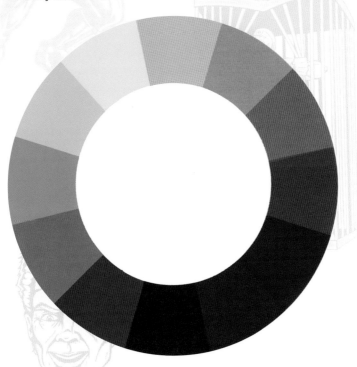

Above: On this colour wheel you can see that the opposite of green is red, blue is orange
and purple is yellow. These opposing colours are what you'll get if you invert an image.

Put to practical use, you can see how colour affects this illustration.

If we colour this main figure in yellow and then keep the background area in a state of orange we see that the figure kind of fades into the background, because these are related colour values.

However, if we take the same image but make the background colour a light shade of purple you can see that the main figure now jumps off the page – due to the benefits of complementary colouring. This simple action helps the figure stand out from the background.

REFINING SKILLS

The following projects will help you become aware of the more advanced traditional methods and terminology.

Stippling

Stippling to add tone and shade is simply a matter of using a very fine-line pen or quill and drawing a series of small lines in the same direction, varying their spacing.

Cross-hatching

You can also use cross-hatching (see page 65) with a quill or pen to add shadow and form. Start with a pretty straightforward sketch of somebody's alter ego.

The drawing appears a little flat because it's essentially 'lit' from the front, as if the subject is flooded with light from a stationary light. This eliminates all the shadows and almost all sense of form.

With this one a bit of loose crosshatching is added to the right-hand side of the portrait to emphasise form – as if the light were now coming from stage left and above.

Setting the light source low is a great choice if you want to create a spooky mood or suggest eerie lighting.

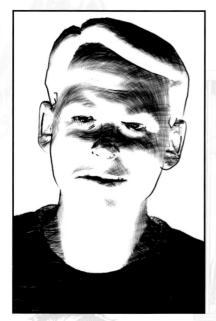

With this one there's a much stronger light stage left, throwing heavy black shadows to the right – still following the contours of the face.

Working in coloured pencil

Traditional blending is accomplished with waxy-style coloured pencils by applying one colour over another and then rubbing the colours with a cotton swab or a stump.

Left: A stump is a tool used to blend pencil lines.

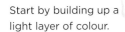

Start by building up a light layer of colour.

Then build up a layer of colour on top of the base; this will be effective in creating a sense of tone in the work that you can't get any other way.

Choosing the style of paper is equally important – a smooth finish will give you a very different feel from a more toothy watercolour-type paper. Ordinary drawing paper is fine for practice and getting familiar with the feel of your pencils.

With water-based coloured pencils you can take a damp brush (just make sure it's only damp, not wet) and manipulate the colours as you would with watercolour. This works best when you're working on watercolour paper.

PHOTOSHOP CS4

Digital artwork is increasing in popularity every day. Photoshop comes with information about technique, but this digested project will help you get the best from the program.

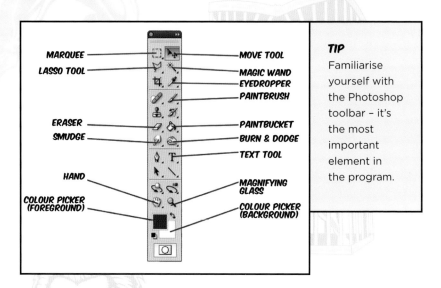

MARQUEE

LASSO TOOL

MOVE TOOL

MAGIC WAND

EYEDROPPER

PAINTBRUSH

ERASER

SMUDGE

PAINTBUCKET

BURN & DODGE

TEXT TOOL

HAND

MAGNIFYING GLASS

COLOUR PICKER (FOREGROUND)

COLOUR PICKER (BACKGROUND)

TIP
Familiarise yourself with the Photoshop toolbar – it's the most important element in the program.

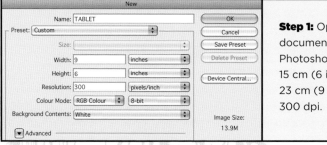

Step 1: Open a new document in Photoshop. Make it 15 cm (6 in) high by 23 cm (9 in) wide, at 300 dpi.

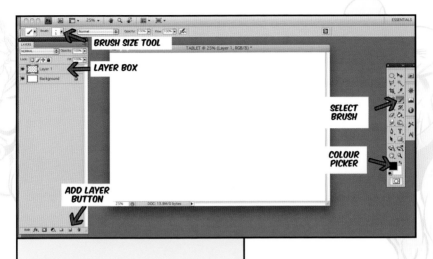

BRUSH SIZE TOOL

LAYER BOX

SELECT BRUSH

COLOUR PICKER

ADD LAYER BUTTON

Step 2: In the Layer box, add a new layer. Make sure the Colour Picker is set as black and choose a paintbrush size of five pixels.

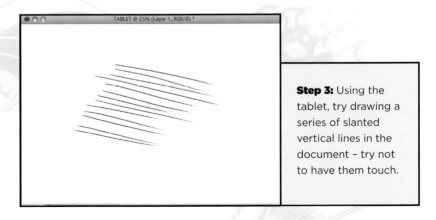

Step 3: Using the tablet, try drawing a series of slanted vertical lines in the document – try not to have them touch.

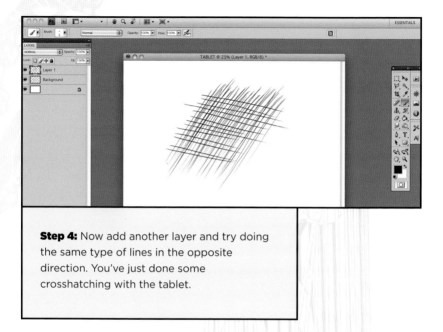

Step 4: Now add another layer and try doing the same type of lines in the opposite direction. You've just done some crosshatching with the tablet.

Digital portrait

Now try to sketch something (or in this case, someone).

Step 1: Open a new document – same as before and add a new layer. This time set the colour at light blue, using the Colour Picker. Keep the same size paintbrush as before (five pixels).

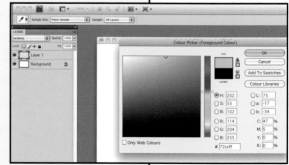

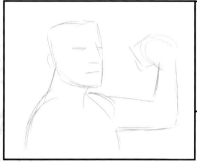

Step 2: Loosely sketch in the basic shapes you would draw if you were doing a head-and-shoulders portrait of a person.

Step 3: Work in some lines and shapes to make up the face – not too much detail, you can add that in a moment.

Step 4: Now add a layer and change the Colour Picker to black – then zoom in so you can start drawing in the facial details.

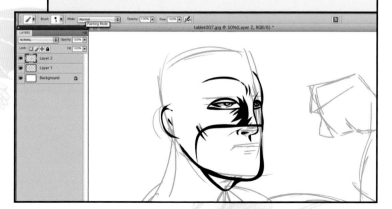

Step 5: Keep working those details using the Paintbrush tool: eyes, hair... you know what to do.

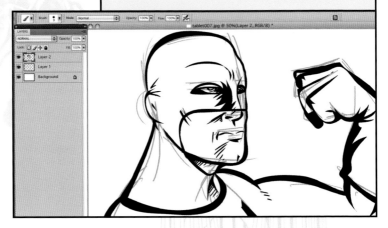

Step 6: When you are finished, delete the layer with the light blue lines and bam! – finished digital portrait, done.

Adding colour

Hold on a minute – what about colour? Well if you wanted to colour this piece in traditional comic book style (flat colour), you can do that pretty easily too.

Step 1: With the portrait still open, add a layer to the drawing and then drag it under the black outline layer.

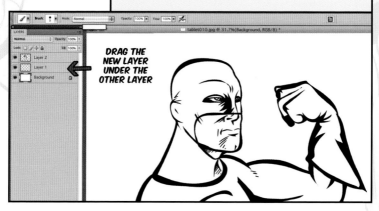

Step 2: Name this layer 'Colour'. Choose a flesh colour using the Colour Picker and select a 45pt brush. Working on the colour layer (which is underneath the black line layer) you can begin to paint the colour in, zooming in if you need to.

Step 3: : The nice thing about this process is that because the black is on a separate layer you can add the colour in and not worry about covering the black lines. Go through the same process to add more colours and pretty soon you'll have a fully coloured image.

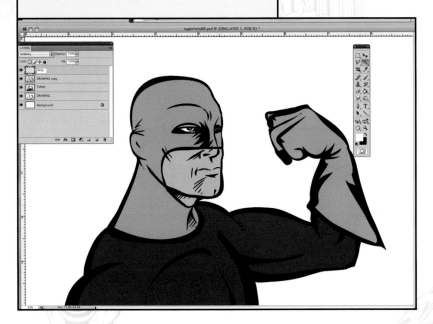

CLICK ON THE BLUE TAB TO CHANGE IT FROM 'NORMAL' TO 'MULTIPLY'

TIP

Create a shadow effect by adding yet another layer over the colour layer – call this one 'Grey' and select a grey colour with the Colour Picker.

Colour in a grey shadow right on top of the colours – use the eraser to sharpen up the edges.

Now for the cool part – go to the Layer box and select the grey layer. Now go up to the top and change the layer style from Normal to Multiply...

... and this gives you a darker shade of colour just like a real shadow.

Adding digital backgrounds

Many artists now use the 'cel' method to create their backgrounds, so named because of the technique used in classic animation when an artist would paint a background and then, on a separate clear piece of acetate, they would paint or colour the individual figures, allowing them to move the character without changing the background.

One method of working this way digitally is to use a photograph that you've taken yourself (you should always use your own photographs instead of something someone else took – you don't want to violate someone's copyright).

Keep the portrait open too; we're going to put the two of them together.

Now in this example I'm using a shot I took in New York City the last time I was there. The background doesn't have to be buildings – it could be wilderness, outer space (good luck taking that picture) or it could be inside your house – it really doesn't matter.

Step 1: Click on the 'Photo' layer so that it's the one Photoshop is focused on and now go to Image>Adjustment>Hue/Saturation and move the scroll bars around until you get an interesting colour scheme.

Step 2: Over to the portrait. Go to Layer>Flatten image.

TIP

Try bringing the Opacity Level down on the layer that holds your digital background. Bringing it to 70–80% will cause it to fade and your primary figure to pop.

Step 3: Select the Magic Wand tool and click it in the white part of the portrait – you'll see the 'marching ants', those crazy dotted lines that mean you've selected all the white areas.

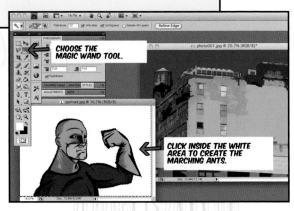

CHOOSE THE MAGIC WAND TOOL.

CLICK INSIDE THE WHITE AREA TO CREATE THE MARCHING ANTS.

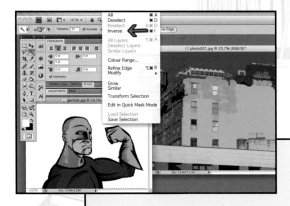

Step 4: Go to Select>Inverse and you'll see the ants now surround the portrait outline.

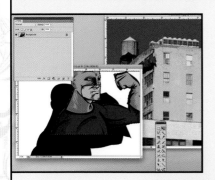

Step 5: Use the Move tool to grab the image inside the marching ant area – you'll see that it changes from a crosshair symbol to a tiny pair of scissors. Hold your mouse down and drag the image over to your other canvas with the buildings in the background.

Step 6: You can move the portrait image around and place it where you want it in the background.

Chapter 2

Developing style

SUPERHEROES EMCOMPASS A VARIETY OF STYLES AND GENRES. FIND OUT WHAT CHARACTER STYLES ARE AVAILABLE TO YOU WHEN STARTING OUT WITH HEROES AND VILLAINS.

SUPERHERO DESIGN

Some artists, like Jack Kirby or John Romita Jr, work with big blocky characters whilst others, like Mike Mignola or Ryan Sook, work with shadows and mood. Still others work in the Japanese or 'Manga' style... In this chapter we take a generic superhero costume – mask, cape and bright colour scheme – and render it in range of styles.

Left: Here's our basic superhero character, rendered in a rather bland way ready for costume details.

Cubism

The broadest sense of comic book style instantly brings up thoughts of Jack Kirby, whose blocky, powerful style was essential to the success of Marvel Comics in the 1960s and was mimicked by Frank Miller in his landmark Batman: The Dark Knight Returns, in 1986. This particular style puts an emphasis on power.

You can see how blocky this particular style is when you break it down into basic shapes. Note that by positioning the head in a different direction to the chest it is possible to keep the figure from looking stiff.

The strongest elements, when working in this style, are the hands and the head of the figure, with a concentration on gesture and broad strokes. You shouldn't get caught up with too many details when working in the cubism style.

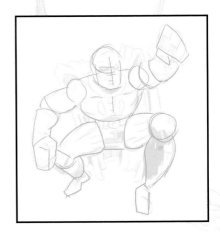

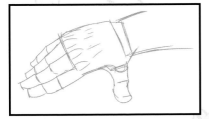

Above: For the hand use big, blocky shapes with wide fingers. There are no delicate lines on cubism-style superheroes; everything is bold.

Above: The face and head also look like they've been chiselled from stone. Heavy brows and flat noses lead to deep-sunk eye sockets, giving the face a very solid, heavy feel.

Realism

At the opposite end of the spectrum to Jack Kirby and others working in his style are artists whose work focuses on reality rather than exaggeration. In the 1940s, artists like Lou Fine and Frank Frazetta led the way towards a more realistic-style comic book art, but it was Neal Adams in the late 1960s and early 1970s who combined that realism with a dynamic edge.

When you break Adams' work down to shapes you can see that he doesn't work in large chunky blocks, like Kirby; instead he uses cylinders and circles whilst maintaining more realistic proportions both for the base figure and musculature.

His figure work is much more fluid and natural. Adams has said that he modelled his Batman figure on martial artist Bruce Lee, who had, like the fictional Batman, trained his body to the peak of physical perfection.

You can see the similarity of Adams' style of figure with this poster from Bruce Lee's film *Game of Death*. Most martial-artist style heroes would have this type of build rather than that of a body builder.

© Columbia Pictures

Manga

Mangaka, or Japanese comic book artists, have developed a style all their own.

Left: They take comics seriously in Japan, as this museum devoted to the 'godfather' of Manga, Osamu Tezuka, in Kyoto, Japan, demonstrates.

Some Manga artists, like Osamu Tezuka (creator of *Astro Boy* and one of the founding fathers of Manga), developed a style that combined a sense of cartooning with outstanding storytelling.

At first glance his artwork seems very simple, almost Disney-like in its appearance.

It's only on closer inspection and with an understanding of subtle technique that we can see his style is achieved by using simple shapes with cartoon proportions, combined with a masterful understanding of body language and emotion through the use of expression.

Modern *mangaka* have injected realism into the more usual cartoon elements of traditional Manga, as shown in this modern retelling of Tekuza's *Astro Boy* series by Naoki Urasawa, *Pluto*.

To work in this more modern Manga style you need to understand the combination of shapes used to create characters.

Above: A jacket for *Astro Boy*, created in 1952 by Osamu Tezuka.

Right: The figure is broken into simplified shapes that follow the rules of both the more cartoony style and the realistic style – so you can see broader shapes with this method.

Minimalism

Working with a simpler style of line is appealing to a lot of artists. Alex Toth, David Mazzucchelli, Chris Ware and a host of other notable artists work in this style. Most were inspired by Noel Sickles, an artist who mastered the deceptively simple limited line technique.

Above: *Scorchy Smith* by Noel Sickles.

The key is to retain an element of realism in the work whilst putting down as few lines as possible, to keep it looking very clean.

Noel Sickles uses a brush to get a rich, smooth line. His faces and figures are realistically depicted but the sketchy line with realistic shadows keeps it minimalist. Let's see what an example of Sickles' artwork would possibly look like if he were to draw our hero.

When you break the figure-work down into shapes you can see that in order to work in this style the anatomical proportions should be realistic – and the pose should be too – there are no exaggerations when you're working in this style.

It's equally important to understand how shadows fall when working in this style – if you break down the drawing one step further, showing the heavily shadowed areas, this becomes even more apparent.

Left, below left and below: A Noel Sickles drawing reworked for the purposes of demonstration.

Expressionism

Expressionist style starts from minimalism and stretches and twists it, defining a look all of its own. It is most apparent in work by Frank Miller in his Sin City series. Characters are defined with blocks like we saw with Kirby's work (see page 88) and the heavy black shadows of Sickles (see page 95). Expressionism is about finding the emotion you are trying to show (or express!) and interpreting it in the illustration.

Right: If you look at the shapes used to make up this figure you can see that we've used the big exaggerated block shapes, but with an over-exaggerated sense of design and posing.

An artist like Bill Sienkiewicz works in an almost abstract style that captures the spirit and energy of the moment. His use of line appears very loose at first glance, but on closer inspection you can see that he is choosing his lines very carefully and that each one complements the illustration. In order to achieve this style, begin with a realistic underdrawing and then work up the form and shadow using broad line strokes.

Working in this style it's important to understand the form and planes of a face, so that they become abstract shapes themselves.

Stylised realism

This is defined by a combination of realistic proportions and shadows and tiny feathering techniques on the dark edges – artists like Art Adams and Brian Bolland work in this style. It's a slightly more graphic design take on the minimalist style.

Stylised abstraction

Artists like Mike Mignola follow the same stylistic path. Mignola uses an advanced knowledge of light and shadow to create a particular atmosphere in his work, adding a layer of moodiness that fits darker subjects perfectly.

Working in this style involves using abstract flat shapes to compose the figure work and then a thorough understanding of shadow to emphasise the form.

Brushwork

Artists like Berni Wrightson, Gene Colan and Kelly Jones work with an inky brush style that keeps the style loose whilst also creating a great sense of atmosphere. Using the brush in this way gives long, feathered lines that you couldn't get any other way, resulting in a somewhat classic, almost old-fashioned illustration style.

Good brushwork can't be duplicated with a pen – those lush, flowing lines that go from thin to thick to thin again and give the illustration a stronger sense of form and a richer sense of detail than any pen could possibly create.

Above and right: Details from Pirates of Mars – a graphic novel series from J.J. Kahrs and Veronica Fish.

Although it takes a great deal of practice to master a brush, it's well worth putting the time in because once you do master this technique, you'll quickly learn that working with a brush is about five times faster than working with a pen.

Getting started with the brush

Take the brush (a No. 2 round was used in the example shown) and dip it in the ink well. Take a scrap piece of paper and practise making lines. If you are right-handed you should work from left to right – resting your wrist on the paper gently and making smooth gesture strokes with the brush, all in the same left-to-right direction. Try to put even pressure on each stroke so that you end up with virtually the same line over and over again.

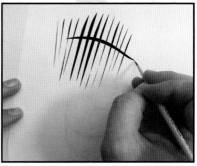

Now, once those lines have dried, and it will only take about a minute, turn the paper round 90° and create some crossing lines. This time, apply some pressure as you move the brush and then let up – this will give you a thin-to-thick line. Experiment with the amount of pressure you use and work up a series of lines. Working in this method will help you gain control of the brushline.

Chapter 3

Types of superhero bodies

COMIC BOOK SUPERHEROES CAN BE SMALL, MEDIUM, LARGE OR EXTRA-LARGE – DEPENDING ON THE CHARACTER AND YOUR IMAGINATION.

SUPERHERO BODIES

In this chapter we'll walk through the basic elements to make up each of these figures – then you can jump over to Chapter 6 when you're ready to add costume details to them.

Shapes

No matter what style you decide to work in, there will be an element of exaggeration to the anatomy.

It's important to understand the basics of anatomy and how we can 'bulk up' the individual muscle areas convincingly.

Let's look at the way this works with a human figure.

Starting with this quick sketch of a normal-sized figure (see page 105, top), you can see that this particular figure is athletic – he's no lightweight; his torso builds up to his broad shoulders. You can see the shapes used to make the figure in the sketch – the same way we did our figure-work in the previous chapter.

It's more than just the figure's size, though – look at his stance – his feet are placed together and he seems pretty casual.

Now with this second figure (see page 105, bottom left) we've used the same method of using shape to build up the figure, but we've increased his muscle

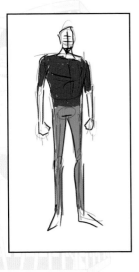

size a great deal. Notice that his feet are spread apart, giving him a sense of heft and his head sits lower on his shoulders – indicating that this guy is more muscle-bound than the previous version.

We can take it up a notch and make that muscle-bound guy look comparatively scrawny, by exaggerating the muscles even further (see below right). We're still basing our figure on simple shapes and following the rules of the ways muscles interact in terms of anatomy, but the muscle groups are super-sized.

There's not much realism in this type of figure, but it's effective as a way of creating a being who could move planets with a sneeze.

Anatomy

This is especially important in the superhero genre because so many superheroes wear costumes that look like they are painted on.

Let's look at the way this works with a human figure.

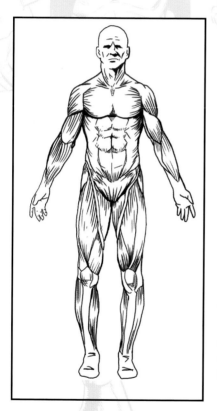

Take a quick look at this figure without the muscle names and concentrate on the way the muscles interact with each other. Note the form lines, which indicate which way the muscles go in the first place. The chest muscles come out from under the shoulder muscles along with the collarbone muscles (the only ones that go horizontally across the body; the rest all flow vertically).

Some important things to notice: the Biceps face the front of the figure whilst the triceps wrap around the back and the shoulders define the upper shape of the bicep muscle.

The upper leg is made up of three major muscles, which give it definition – the Vastus Lateralis and the External Oblique are the most prominent of these.

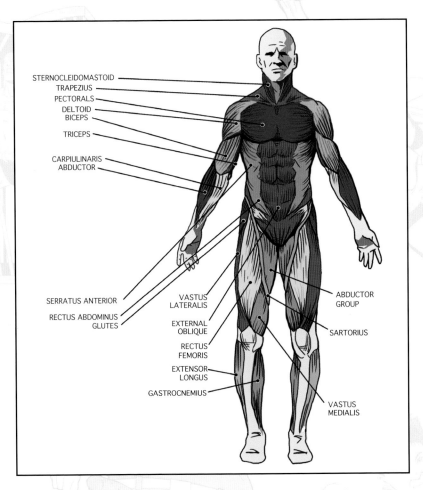

STERNOCLEIDOMASTOID
TRAPEZIUS
PECTORALS
DELTOID
BICEPS

TRICEPS

CARPIULINARIS
ABDUCTOR

SERRATUS ANTERIOR
RECTUS ABDOMINUS
GLUTES

VASTUS
LATERALIS

EXTERNAL
OBLIQUE

RECTUS
FEMORIS

EXTENSOR
LONGUS

GASTROCNEMIUS

ABDUCTOR
GROUP

SARTORIUS

VASTUS
MEDIALIS

Above: When we break the muscles down by colour to make them stand out it becomes much more apparent just how many muscles make up the figure.

From the back you can see there is an equally complex arrangement of muscles.

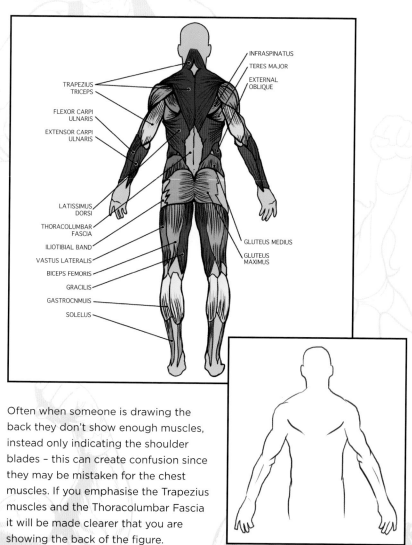

INFRASPINATUS
TERES MAJOR
EXTERNAL
OBLIQUE
TRAPEZIUS
TRICEPS
FLEXOR CARPI
ULNARIS
EXTENSOR CARPI
ULNARIS
LATISSIMUS
DORSI
THORACOLUMBAR
FASCIA
ILIOTIBIAL BAND
VASTUS LATERALIS
BICEPS FEMORIS
GRACILIS
GASTROCNMUIS
SOLELUS
GLUTEUS MEDIUS
GLUTEUS
MAXIMUS

Often when someone is drawing the back they don't show enough muscles, instead only indicating the shoulder blades – this can create confusion since they may be mistaken for the chest muscles. If you emphasise the Trapezius muscles and the Thoracolumbar Fascia it will be made clearer that you are showing the back of the figure.

The female figure

The female figure shares many of the same muscle groups and they interact much the same way as they do on the male, but they tend to be smaller in size and much smoother overall.

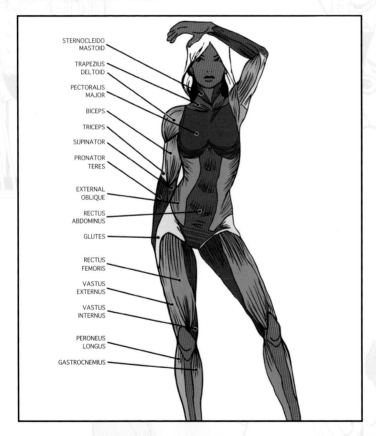

STERNOCLEIDO MASTOID

TRAPEZIUS DELTOID

PECTORALIS MAJOR

BICEPS

TRICEPS

SUPINATOR

PRONATOR TERES

EXTERNAL OBLIQUE

RECTUS ABDOMINUS

GLUTES

RECTUS FEMORIS

VASTUS EXTERNUS

VASTUS INTERNUS

PERONEUS LONGUS

GASTROCNEMIUS

Take note of the way the Deltoid (shoulder) muscle interacts with the Bicep when the arm is raised. The muscles not only interact with each other, but they also move together, stretching and pulling.

The muscled figure

He's muscular but not muscle-bound.

Left: Captain Triumph is a great example of a muscled male hero.

Step 1: Start out with the simple shapes you've already used to make a figure. You're going to bulk up his arm and leg muscles by using wider cylinders. For the chest, use a more pronounced V-shape to emphasise his wide shoulders and strong pecs.

Step 2: Tighten up the sketchy lines and start to build up the form details of the figure.

Step 3: Refine details such as those in the face. No mask for this character and the kind of hairstyle that blows with the gentle wind. Give him a little bit of a smile, too.

Step 4: Work in some of the details of the rest of his body – switch to a darker, softer pencil lead to refine some of these lines.

Step 5: Use a small, fine white eraser to clean up some of the sketchy lines so that you can get a cleaner look at the figure. You'll work in the details of his costume later in Chapter 6.

The lean, muscled hero

This is often the body type of the urban crusader or the antihero – think Bruce Lee-style muscles for this figure.

Left: The Golden-Age Daredevil was a lean fighting machine.

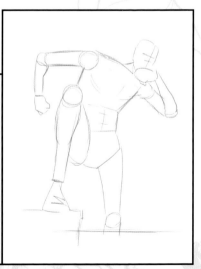

Step 1: Begin with basic figure shapes. This time, have fun with the antihero type – this figure would probably be hunched over. Since he's a leaner figure than before, the cylinders you use to make the figure should be narrower than in the previous example.

Step 2: Work in a few more details and a cape. The cape will be a big part of the character, so it wraps and drapes heavily around him.

Step 3: Start working in some of the final lines using a softer pencil lead. This figure will be heavily cloaked in shadows but you still want to get all of the anatomy correct.

Step 4: A good way to understand how a cape works is by bunching up a 'river' of wrinkles at the neck – by starting at a point under the character's chin and then fanning them out you get a more realistic form.

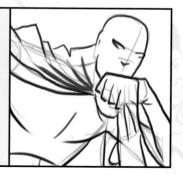

Skip to Chapter 6 to finish the details of the figure.

The skinny hero

This is the body type of sidekicks and teenage adventurers. There's muscle, but it's mostly still in development.

Left: The Kitten was one of the most famous sidekicks of the Golden Age of comics, getting herself into one mess after another – but luckily Cat Man was always nearby.

Step 1: Begin with those same basic shapes to make up the human figure but, because you want the sidekick to be a younger person (sidekicks almost always are), you need to build a smaller figure all the way through. Make the torso a bit thinner – both at the waist and the shoulders. His left arm is going to be reaching towards us so there's a bit of foreshortening there.

Step 2: Tighten up your drawing in pencil. His wide stance makes him appear younger. Keep the neck relatively thick and the head slightly long – both go a long way towards indicating youth.

Step 3: Switch to a darker pencil to focus on the muscle groups – you want to avoid any exaggeration with this figure, so keep all of them very realistically proportioned.

Skip to Chapter 6 to finish the details of the figure.

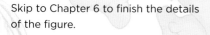

The exaggerated hero

This superhero is unrealistically proportioned. In reality he'd have trouble moving around, never mind performing amazing acts of heroism – but much like a lot of pro wrestlers, this big burly hero is very popular.

Step 1: Look at a 'regular'-sized figure in a heroic pose so you can see how the anatomy works.

Now sketch out the same basic pose but in an exaggerated way.

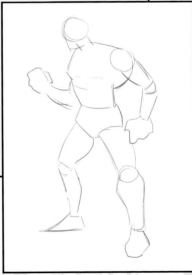

Step 2: Work in the details following the lines you set up in the sketch. His pose is especially important here – you want him to have a stance that indicates his weight. Note that the chest area is much bigger, the shoulders are bigger, he has larger hands and big, thick leg muscles. His proportions stay pretty much the same – you're just making the muscles bigger. Note too the repositioned right foot from the 'regular' sketch.

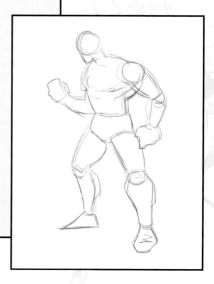

Step 3: Start working in the details of the figure – big, broad muscles. Work in the details on the right hand.

TIP

By drawing sharp, squarish angles for the muscles, you can give the impression of a hard muscle. If you were to draw the same muscles using soft, rounded lines, the muscles would end up looking doughy.

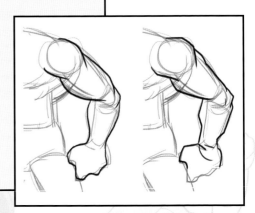

Step 4: Draw in the knuckles on the right hand, then the fingers. Use your own hand as a reference – when you make a fist it's more of a rounded shape than a square one. Work out the wrinkles and the details.

Step 5: Once you're happy with the hand, go over it with a darker lead pencil (here, a 2B pencil was used).

Step 6: Rework the left hand too – loosely sketch in the knuckles and the fingers.

Step 7: Go over the lightly sketched pencil lines and you have a pretty good base figure. Turn to Chapter 6 to finish him off.

Chapter 4

Good, evil and supporting characters

YOU CAN'T HAVE YOUR SUPERHEROES GO UP AGAINST THE LUNCH LADY, CAN YOU? SO YOU NEED TO GIVE SOME THOUGHT TO CREATING WORTHY ADVERSARIES TO SHOW OFF JUST HOW AMAZING YOUR HEROES ARE.

ADVERSARIES

Brutes are often henchmen, assisting the villain with all the heavy lifting, but in recent years the idea of a big, hulking, yet intelligent villain has taken hold in comics and film.

The stupid brute

The original brute – brawn rather than brain is this character's main attribute.

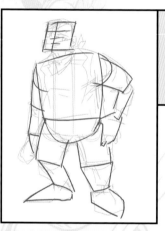

Step 1: Start with the traditional human figure, but with an emphasis on bulk, making your body shapes very square.

Step 2: Working on top of the basic construction lines, add in some details such as the neckerchief and the tattered sports jacket. Note that with this figure, even though he's standing still, his legs are bent at the knees to give the impression of weight and movement.

Step 3: Work in the colours and the black outlines around the figure. Note the darker shade on the chin to indicate a five o'clock shadow. By giving the figure big, hairy hands you can emphasise his size. By leaving a bit of space at the shoulders you also give the impression that his jacket is coming apart. The henchman is often slow-witted and may stand in a timid way despite his immense size, as shown here.

The mastermind brute

A mastermind of brute will not only be big and imposing, but he'll stand more confidently. This type of villain revels in his victories and spends a great deal of his time letting his enemy know how much smarter than them he is.

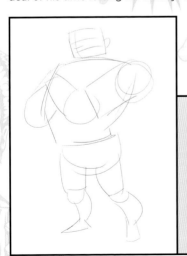

Step 1: Rough in the shapes to make up the figure using a soft pencil – in this case a non-photo red pencil. Because he's a big guy, make his upper body dwarf his lower body. Keeping his head slightly small also adds to his imposing size.

Step 2: Using a blue pencil, work in some of the details of the figure, paying attention to his sinister-looking face, heavy brow and wide, broad chin.

Step 3: Using a brush and ink, quickly go over the more final lines of the drawing. Work in the blacks of the boots, gloves and belt.

Step 4: Allow the ink enough time to dry (at least an hour), then use a soft white eraser to clean up the pencil lines. Scan the drawing into Photoshop at 300 dpi (RGB) or hand colour it using coloured inks.

Step 5: Fill in the basic colours of the figure. In this case, give him evil yellow skin and blue hair – certainly the earmarks of a villain – and a bright-coloured costume. Working in Photoshop do all the colour on a separate layer and set to Multiply so the black lines show through. If you're doing the colour by hand make sure you use a clean, dry brush as you work with each new ink so the colour goes down clean and smooth.

Step 6: If you are working traditionally you will skip this step. In Photoshop, select the layer with the black and white drawing on it. Select the Magic Wand tool and click on the white background outside the figure. As long as you have no open lines in the black and white piece, all of the white area will be selected, shown by the marching ants. Go to Select>Inverse and now the figure itself will be outlined with the ants. Add a new layer called 'Shadows' and use the Paint Bucket tool to fill this area with grey, selected using the Colour Picker. Change the layer to Multiply and you'll have added a dark shadow above the whole figure.

Step 7: To add shadows to the image in the traditional way, simply work up a mixture of roughly 50:50 water and ink and go over the completely dry coloured inks – it's a good idea to let the inks dry for at least two hours before going over them. If you're working in Photoshop go to the Shadow layer you just created and, using the Polygonal Lasso tool, cut into the shadows, emphasising the form of the figure. In this case the figure is backlit so we would see shadow on the front of the character – this adds drama in abundance.

Step 8: Lastly, if you're working traditionally you may want to go over the entire image with ink again using a brush. This gives it a more printed comic book look. If you're working with Photoshop you can accomplish this by going over the drawing with the digital stylus on the tablet.

TIP

Attitude and some creative lighting go a long way towards giving your villain the right amount of menace. It's simply a matter of understanding the planes and form that make up the face or the figure.

Right: A scar adds a bit of character – and take a look at that crazy all-white left eye, too.

Twisted and deranged villain

Bad posture is a common trait amongst villainous characters. Giving them a slouch doesn't necessarily make them evil, but it definitely makes them seem less heroic.

Left: Taking the slouch to the extreme, you end up with the twisted and deranged villain.

Step 1: Start out with the shapes that make up a human figure, but twist the figure into a very uncomfortable position. Here his right leg is intentionally broken and being dragged, as is his right arm. Keep the pencil lines loose.

Step 2: Use a different-coloured pencil to tighten up and refine the details of the figure. A bit of drool, some crazy eyes and a claw-like hand add to his overall twisted nature.

Step 3: Go over the pencil lines with ink using a No. 2 round brush. Being bald seems to be a trait common amongst super-criminals. His Converse trainers betray his fashion sense. After the ink has dried, erase all the pencil lines with a soft white eraser.

Step 4: Scan the image into Photoshop at 300 dpi. Use the Magic Wand tool to select the white around the figure – remember to use the Add To option to select the areas that are segregated, like under his chest and under his left arm. Once all of these areas are selected (shown by the marching ants) choose Select>Inverse to grab the area on top of the figure. Now add a layer and fill it with grey paint using the Paint Bucket tool. Set the layer to Multiply to show the drawing underneath.

Step 5: Lighten the grey slightly by going to Brightness/Contrast and sliding the selector towards the lighter option. Then use the Polygonal Lasso tool to select one side of the figure and hit the delete key – thereby eliminating the grey shadow from one side of the figure. If you'd rather work traditionally you'll want to add a grey wash – but if you are planning on colouring this illustration with ink, add the wash last.

Step 6: If you're working in Photoshop add a layer set to Multiply and fill in the colours; you'll be able to see the grey shadow through the colours.

Jekyll and Hyde-style character

Robert Louis Stevenson's *The Strange Case of Dr Jekyll and Mr Hyde* has captured our imagination since it was first published in 1886. The idea of man's duality and the conflict between good and evil is one that has been adapted into comic book form many times over.

In creating a model sheet for this character, you would actually have to do two separate ones, because you are essentially designing two distinct characters. With model sheets, try to avoid the temptation to be creative with the pose or lighting and opt instead for a very simple pose that is seen straight on. You can incorporate these model sheets into a more dramatic shot later (and you will).

Step 1: Sketch out a rather ordinary human figure using a soft pencil. You want to emphasise the contrast between the two characters, so aim for average here. Note the slanted shoulders.

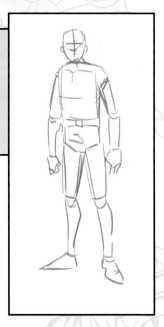

Step 2: Go over those basic form lines with some details, like a shirt and a pair of jeans, by tightening it up with an HB .05 mm pencil. Then use either a quill or brush with some black ink to go over the final lines.

Step 3: Let it dry completely and then erase the pencil lines with a soft white eraser.

Step 4: Either use a brush and some watercolour paint with a mix of two parts paint to one part water (which will give you a more solid colour) or scan the drawing into Photoshop at 300 dpi and fill in the drawing with basic colours.

Step 5: Now, start on his alter ego. Follow the same basic shapes you used to design the ordinary figure, but here you're going to exaggerate everything to make him much bigger.

Step 6: Work in the details the same way you did for the first drawing. The ripped shirt and tattered trousers might not realistically stay on the figure if he really did transform, but in comics you can take some artistic licence.

Step 7: Go over the lines in ink, using the same method as for the previous figure. Let it dry and then erase the pencil lines.

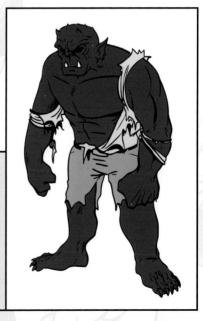

Step 8: Finally, add colour to the model sheet – making certain that whatever is left over from the previous design matches this one – namely the belt and the same shades of blue and yellow for the trousers and shirt.

The transformation

So you're chomping at the bit to make a more exciting illustration of this Jekyll and Hyde character – let's do a transformation scene. If this is the superhero character, expect to do a variation of this scene in just about every story you draw – after all, that's his selling point.

Step 1: The first sketch is to just try and figure out what will be in the illustration. Simply put, you need to see the before and after – the challenge is to make it clear that the character is transforming. This first idea here is too simple, but it's the basis of what we'll illustrate.

Step 2: Go with four stages of the transformation and improve the first stage with a bit more drama – the figure will start with his head in his hands, fall backwards and then step towards the viewer.

Step 3: Tighten up the drawing with an HB .05 mm lead pencil. There are a few important details to take note of – figure two's shirt is starting to come apart at the seams, his hair is dishevelled and it looks like his buttons are bursting.

Step 4: It's important to make sure that figures one through three all appear to be on the same motion line – as if the figure is leaning backwards through the transformation. You can accomplish this by creating an arc that lines up with the character's head at each stage.

Step 5: Using a brush and some black India ink, work in the final details – the eyes in figure two will be strange, so the viewer gets the idea that a change is taking place.

Step 6: Once the inking is finished, let the piece dry completely and then erase the pencil lines using a soft white eraser.

Step 7: Now add some 'energy dots'. Simply draw a series of circles, either freehand, using a template or a compass. The circles should be placed randomly and their sizes varied for an organic feel.

Step 8: Fill in the circles with black ink using a No. 2 round brush. Whilst you're adding this black area, increase the shadows on the figures themselves to add some more drama – concentrating on the shirt on figure one and the face on figure four.

Step 9: Scan the drawing into Photoshop at 300 dpi in RGB mode. Open the file and create a new layer called 'Colours'. Set the layer style to Multiply and start applying colour to the illustration. Notice that the skin colour is turning from its natural state to its transformed colour.

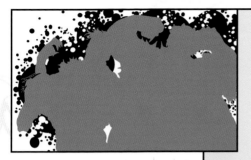

Step 10: Use the Polygonal Lasso tool to select the area around all of the figures. Add a new layer called 'Shadows' and use the Paint Bucket to fill it with grey.

Step 11: Change the layer mode from Normal to Multiply and the image underneath will show through.

Step 12: Still on the Shadow layer, select the Eraser tool. Choose the Brush option at the top of the screen, selecting a 59 Splatter Brush – then bring the Opacity level down to about 15% and start erasing the grey, concentrating on the form of the figures. The light source is from the left, so that means the left side of the figures will have virtually no shadow, whilst the right side will have heavier shadows. Use the Eraser tool slowly and remove the shadows until the image looks dramatic and finished.

Superhero family *by Veronica Fish*

Dating back to the beginning of the comic book industry, the idea of a superhero family has always been a popular one – and it continues today with blockbuster films like *The Incredibles*.

Step 1: Using a blue pencil, sketch out the general body shapes of the superhero family. Keep in mind that everybody is different, so each character gets a distinct feel. Superhero kids shouldn't be too muscular and the super-mum isn't either. The more muscles you give a character, the more masculine it becomes.

Step 2: Using this construction sketch as a guide, move on to the drawing. Form super-dad's square jaw and large calf and arm muscles. Add a cape for movement. Having the dad holding onto the kid's foot and the mum looking towards them smiling are nice details that make them seem like a family.

Step 3: Scan the image into Photoshop and make a new layer. Changing the layer from Normal to Multiply allows you to see the drawing lines underneath. In any base colours you wish, create simple blocks of colour. It's best to start with large areas and work on the details last. With this layer as just a solid mass of colour, you can easily use the Magic Wand tool to go back and select just the figures and colour inside – no more worrying about going outside the lines.

Step 4: Start to define the characters, making sure the father's head isn't lost in too much blue. For a cartoon family, it's a good idea to have at least two members with the same hair colour for easy recognition. For their costumes, it could be fun to use the same colours but not necessarily the same style.

Step 5: Now, using the handy Magic Wand tool, pick up the figures and start to create shadows and highlights. With the Burn and Dodge tools, work in the dark and light areas, making sure the light source is consistent.

Step 6: Put a sky behind the characters. Using the Magic Wand tool, select the area around the figures – now you won't colour over them.

Step 7: Touch up the entire piece, cleaning up stray lines, improving on the details such as belts, boots, hair, hands, masks and so on. Zoom in and make sure everything is the best it can be.

Step 8: Finally, to give a different feel to the piece, make a new layer and fill it completely with a bright colour, such as red. Then change the setting from Normal to Overlay, Hue or Colour. Experiment to see how this brightens up vivid colours and ties all the elements together – like a family!

Superheroine *by Veronica Fish*

The tradition of the superheroine has swiftly overtaken the female sidekick as the ultimate feminine superstar.

Step 1: Loosely sketch out the pose. Keeping the shapes general, build the body. Make sure the proportions are correct at this stage, before going too far into detail. By giving the character such an active pose, she looks super-dynamic and ready for action. The hair will flow in the opposite direction to give more movement.

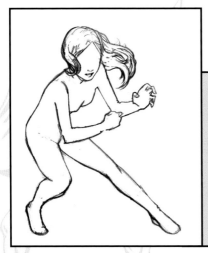

Step 2: After drawing the construction lines, use a lightbox and begin to form the finished drawing. Keep improving the musculature – even if you don't want the character to come across as too buff and masculine – getting the muscles right is important.

Step 3: The next step is to make a bodysuit. The fabric will wrinkle at the elbows and knees, but pull at the chest and extended leg. Short boots are added and more swirling hair. Hair is really fun to draw, as it twists and turns, giving motion and texture to the character. To make it more lifelike, separate the sections of hair and intertwine them.

Step 4: Finish the look of the costume. Small details like seams, buttons, zippers or laces make a big difference. This character will also get some cool fingerless driver's gloves and heart-shaped knee pads. A mask is added and the eyes are taken away. You can experiment with which parts of the face you'd like to show. You can choose to keep the eyes showing through the holes, for example, for a different feel.

Step 5: Scan the finished drawing into Photoshop at 300 dpi. Make a new layer and set it to Multipy. Block in big sections of colour; it will make it easier to select large areas to colour. To go with the heart knee pads, go with a bright pink all over, defining which parts of the skin will be exposed.

Step 6: That was a bit too much pink, so scale it back. Using the Magic Wand tool, select the pink on the layer with the colour and select Brush using a nice, icy grey. With a grey just a few shades darker, you can put in some good shadows. By keeping the costume details in pink, she has a neat pop of bright colour.

Step 7: Now you can move onto the easy stuff. Select the Burn tool, set the brush to a big and fluffy tip and sweep over the shadows to add some depth. Choose the Dodge tool and set it to a smaller tip but still with fluffy edges. Keeping the light source consistent, add some highlights to the costume. Highlighting details on the bridge of the nose and the sides of the cheeks is a great touch.

Step 8: Finish up all the rough edges of the piece. Zoom in to touch up the fingers, shoe details and any sloppy bits. To give a colourful pop, make a new layer and set it to Screen. Drop in a navy blue and watch the black lines turn into a sweet, saturated blue.

SUPERPORTING CAST

You can't have a great superhero without a great supporting cast – secret identities, snooping girlfriends, angry bosses and clueless relatives are all good context-givers.

The housekeeper or kindly aunt

She's usually wondering where the hero runs off to every time there is an emergency...

Step 1: Start with some basic doughy shapes – having the hip area larger than the chest area gives her a nice look.

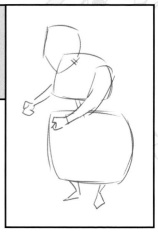

Step 2: Flesh out the details using a soft lead pencil. Her tiny feet will add character.

Step 3: Start going over the rough lines with ink and a No. 2 brush. Her posture and the idea that she has a vest over her sweater betray the fact that she's an older woman.

Step 4: Adding a pattern to her vest will add some details to the figure.

Step 5: Finish off the tray and add a pair of glasses.

Step 6: Scan her into Photoshop at 300 dpi. Add a new layer and colour the illustration. Giving the shoulder opening a hot-pink flare shows off her fun side. Note the white highlights in her grey hair too.

Step 7: She looks a bit too sad, so zoom in and use a very small (No. 5) brush to change her frown into a small smile. Give her lips a bit of pink.

Step 8: Add a new layer and drop in some shadows, keeping the layer set to Multiply. Adding the smiley face badge shows that she has personality.

The boss

The boss might be a volatile police captain or a crusading daily newspaper editor – he's a figure of authority and power.

Step 1: Start with some blocky shapes and keep the lines loose using a soft coloured pencil. Draw lightly to save on erasing. He's going to have some bulk, especially in his upper body area, with his legs somewhat thinner and his mid-section a little bit doughy.

Step 2: Tighten up the drawing a bit, working in some of the details you learned in the muscle lessons (see pages 104–119). You want to give the impression that he was once very big and athletic but he's now getting a little soft. Use a rounder method of showing the muscles this time.

Step 3: Skip the regular pencil tightening and work right from the loose sketch. With a No. 2 round brush and some India ink, begin working in the details on the boss, concentrating on his face first. He's going to be an older, 'seasoned', veteran so give him a few wrinkles and a receding hairline. Big bushy eyebrows give him an air of authority.

Step 4: Work up the rest of the figure, giving him all-black trousers and a loosened tie along with rolled up shirtsleeves, to make it clear that he's a working man.

Step 5: Let the ink dry fully and erase the pencil lines using a soft white eraser.

Step 6: Scan the image into Photoshop at 300 dpi. Add a new layer called 'Colour'. Change it from Normal to Multiply and colour the boss using some fairly straightforward colours.

Step 7: Add a new layer called 'Shadows', select a medium/light grey using the Colour Picker and add some shadows to the figure.

Step 8: Using a Splatter Brush (around 43 px) work in some shadows, following most of the lines already established. Select the Eraser tool (21 px), bring the Opacity down to 15% and erase some of the shadows you've just drawn in – this gives them a nice, uneven, more natural feel. Change the Shadow layer from Normal to Multiply and the shadows will fill in nicely.

Step 9: The boss's role will vary depending on your story. Follow the instructions on pages 82–5 to learn how to place him in a setting.

SECRET IDENTITIES

All good superheroes have secret identities, but when you break it down they really fall into only three categories.

- The millionaire – a wealthy industrialist, man (or woman) about town who fights crime for a hobby. His wealth explains how he can take the time off to go on his crusades.

- The working man – usually a reporter or some other 'white collar' type of job. There have been many attempts at making an artist the alter ego of a superhero and even a couple of instances where the crime fighter's secret ID was that of a policeman.

- The student – this goes all the way back to the days of Captain Marvel from Fawcett comics. The student has to balance grades and crime fighting.

The student

The polar opposite of the confident millionaire, the student should almost always be panicked – he's new to the superhero game.

Step 1: You know the drill – loose cylinder-type shapes – put him in a running position as if he's ready for action, but he's looking the wrong way when he runs (he's nervous).

Step 2: Tighten up the figure work and clothes with an HB .05 mm pencil. He's young, so you need to use a few tricks to show this: slightly gangly body, thin neck, as well as a more youthful choice of clothing.

Step 3: Finish the pencil work – his face still has 'baby fat' cheeks as another indicator of his age. He also has a very weak chin.

Step 4: Use a No. 2 round brush and some India ink to go over the pencil lines with ink. By putting his left leg in shadow you can indicate the form. Let the ink dry thoroughly and then scan it into Photoshop at 300 dpi.

Step 5: Here's a neat trick to draw the laces on the character's trainers. Add a new layer and call it 'Laces'. Go to Layer>Layer style>Stroke (located at the top of the screen) and the Layer style box will pop up.

Adjust the size to 3 and make sure the chosen colour is black. Now choose a 5 px brush with white, make sure you have selected the Laces layer (it will be highlighted in blue) and draw a row of laces.

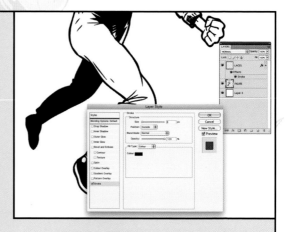

Go to Layer> Duplicate layer and you will have a second layer of laces. Use the Polygonal Lasso tool to draw a box over the laces you've just drawn.

Hit the delete key – it won't look like anything happened, but you've just eliminated the second set of laces.

Stay on the Laces copy layer, use the Brush (again, 5 px with white) and draw in the bow.

Because that layer is above the other layer the bow will look as if it's above the row of laces.

Step 6: Add a new layer called 'Colours', change the Opacity setting for the layer from Normal to Multiply and fill in the colours of the character.

Working with a digital tablet

There is a wide range of graphics tablets to choose from. An economical 10 x 15 cm (4 x 6 in) tablet such as the Wacom Bamboo will cost you about £40 whilst a top-of-the-line extra-large tablet will cost you about £4,000 – the small one is an excellent choice, though, and works well for the beginner and the experienced digital artist alike.

Left: A digital tablet.

Step 7: Try something different to indicate highlights and shadows on the figure. Making sure you're on the Colours layer, choose the Dodge tool on the toolbar.

Change the Dodge tool settings (on the bar above the work area) to a 59 px Splatter Brush with an exposure of 9%. Now take the brush and work the Dodge tool in the colour area – you'll see wherever you touch lightens the area. 'Dodge' is a photographic term used in a darkroom when light is added to a certain area of a developing photograph.

Step 8: Underneath the Dodge tool is the Burn tool (remember, if you want to know what a tool is, just leave the mouse over it and a little popup will tell you its name). The Burn tool works in the opposite way to the Dodge tool – it darkens whatever area it touches. Use the Burn tool to create shadow on the opposite side of the figure.

Chapter 5

Emotion and motion

YOUR SUPERHEROES NEED TO BE FOLLOWED WITH ADORATION OR FEAR. IN ORDER FOR THIS TO WORK YOU NEED THEM TO PORTRAY REALISTIC EMOTION AND MOTION.

EMOTION

Emotion is very important in superhero comics, as demonstrated by this great cover for *Hangman Comics* from 1942.

Left: The Hangman's stern expression tells you something about this character's grim nature.

Capturing emotion is a key component of successfully placing the superheroes in credible situations. Take a look at the emotions opposite.

There are very subtle differences between some of them and whilst they may look similar, the differences are what make them stand out.

For example, 'fear' and 'surprise' are very similar at first glance, but when you look closer you can see that they really are different. Whilst both have raised eyebrows, open mouth and wide-opened eyes, 'surprise' takes the expressions to a more extreme level – the mouth and eyes are opened wider, giving the impression of real shock.

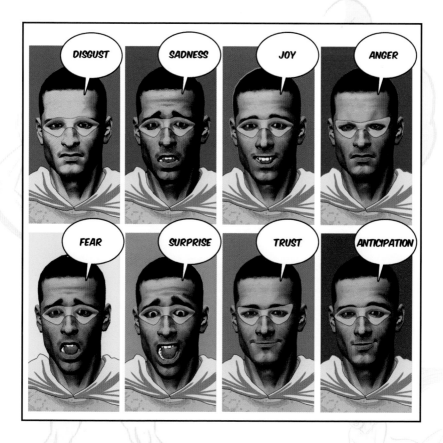

'Disgust' has slightly puckered lips and a softer look to the eyes than the somewhat similar 'anger'.

'Trust' presents a confident smile, whilst 'anticipation' has a little smirk to show his excitement at whatever he is seeing.

'Sadness' and 'joy' are related, but the mouth curves down with 'sadness' and up with 'joy'. Studying these differences will help you to effectively convey emotion in your own drawings.

Advanced emotion

You can combine the subtleties of each emotion to convey more complex emotions.

Right: The emotions work like a maths equation when you combine them – 'fear' and 'surprise' are very much alike; if you take elements from both and tone it down a notch, you get 'awe'.

Sometimes something as simple as a minor curve of the mouth or a slightly raised eyebrow is enough to change a character's emotion. There is a lot of power in subtlety.

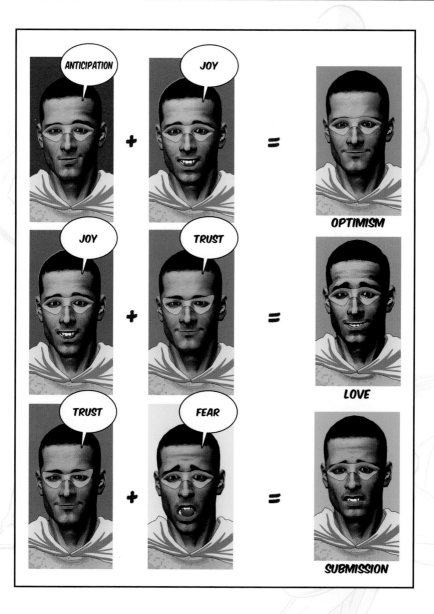

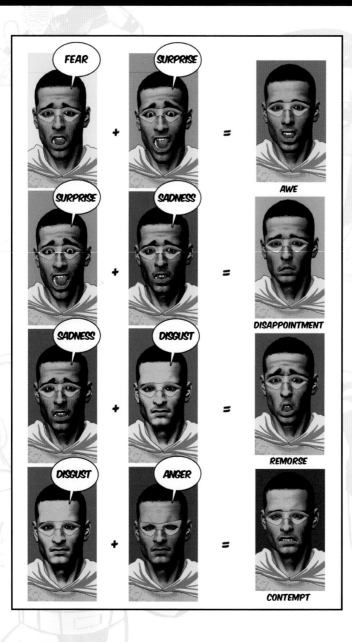

You can see from this diagram that a human arm is capable of quite a wide range of motion – certainly more than 12 positions, but let's use that number to study the range.

Position one shows the arm resting at the figure's side. By position six it is halfway through the motion and the arm is extended straight out. The important thing to note with these first six positions is that the shoulder remains in the lower position throughout the movement.

In position seven, you can see that the shoulder shifts upward slightly and continues to move with the remaining positions until it rests, nearly touching the neck, at position twelve.

You can also see that by position ten the hand has inverted its direction and the elbow begins to bend.

Understanding the basic range of movement is helpful when you want to draw a figure in action. Any moving figure follows these same rules of motion; the movement appears fluid and 'correct'. In this example the figure turns at the waist and the right arm drops as the left arm throws a punch. Note also the feet, which seem to 'slide' into position.

TIP

One way to ensure the action looks correct is to create a 'swoosh line' and then have an element of the figure follow this line – in the example above it's the figure's left shoulder and fist.

If you break this sequence down into separate poses you can see that the left fist follows a trajectory that sticks to the rules of the motion possibilities of the arm. The figure also 'steps into' the punch.

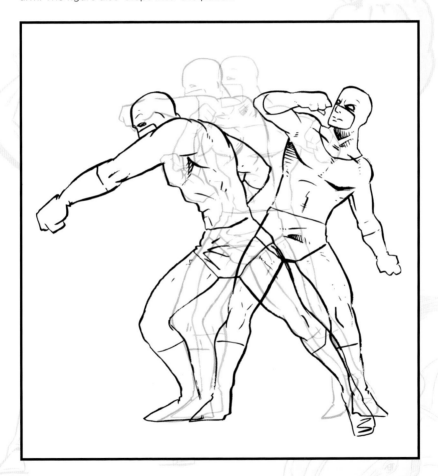

When you're choosing a pose for your superhero, go for the most dramatic – in this example that would be either the first figure or the last, since each one demonstrates extreme ends of the motion spectrum.

Fight scenes

There's no way around it – if you're going to draw superheroes you're going to draw fight scenes. In fact, the superhero etiquette when two heroes meet is to fight, each one usually mistaking the other for a villain... So let's get to it.

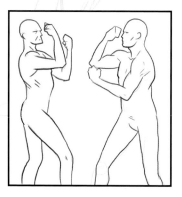

Left: Whilst this pose might be perfect for a pair of Victorian-era brawlers following the Marquess of Queensbury rules of pugilism, it's totally unrealistic for our needs. Superhero poses should be exaggerated and explosive.

Let's take a look at a vintage comic book issue featuring Pyroman slugging some Nazi soldiers.

Even though the figure work is pretty stiff, which was common for comics in the 1940s, there is a lot of energy in this cover art. There's power behind the punch and the dent in the Nazi soldier's helmet makes it clear that this really hurt.

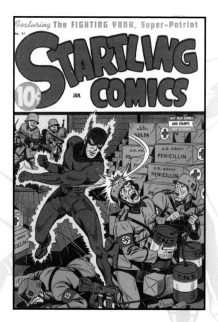

Breaking it down into basic figure shapes, we can get a better idea of how these figures are put together.

In this second take, the character poses are still realistic, but they've taken on a bit more of an exaggerated feel – more like two super-powered beings squaring off.

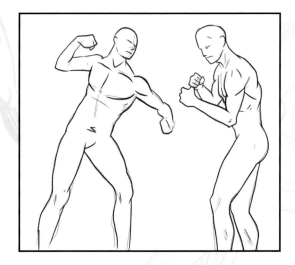

If we take it to the limit we see a real superhero square-off – these figures are posed like no regular humans would ever pose... but then there's nothing 'regular' about a superhero, is there?

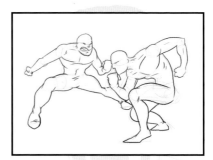

The figures being posed low to the ground gives a sense of intensity. The same goes for the actual fight itself – in reality a pair of boxers throwing punches looks like this:

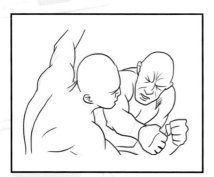

We can see that the first fighter's fist is connecting with the second fighter and we can almost feel his nose caving in, but the punch seems pedestrian. It might be based on reality but, like the example we saw earlier, it lacks drama and impact.

By changing the positioning of the figures as well as the impact the punch is having, we can create a much more dramatic version of the same scene.

With this one, the fighter being hit seems to be getting knocked off his feet. It's a powerful punch and the reader really feels that.

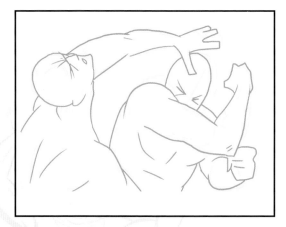

Left: This one takes it even further – the fighter being hit is getting knocked out of the picture.

It's all about how extreme you decide to take it, but remember, overacting is almost always more dramatic when you're trying to show action.

Using the shape method of assembling a figure (see pages 104–119), try drawing different fighting positions – remembering the limitations of the human figure whilst you work. Experimentation is key. Stretch your imagination, watch some Bruce Lee films, take in a boxing match and bring your sketchbook – all of this and more will make you a better artist.

Right: Never bring a knife to a flamethrower fight – as this cover of Airboy shows. There is conflict between the two figures and great dramatic poses show that these are two characters about to mix things up – try to capture that energy in your own work.

Romance

Romance is an important part of your superhero's life – almost to a fault they all have snoopy girlfriends who are constantly trying to figure out their secret identities or getting themselves mixed up in trouble.

TIP

Take a look at the shapes that make up the female figure.

Above: Romance and love comics have a long history, being a popular genre before the emergence of daytime-television soap operas.

The chest and shoulders are narrower than for a male, the waist is higher, making the legs a bit longer and you'll want to work in that hourglass shape.

Romantic trysts *by Veronica Fish*

Think about the kind of person your hero should be with. Are they the quirky, spunky, kind? Or maybe mysterious and quiet? Opposites attract, but sometimes they hate each other. Try to create a significant other that complements your hero; you can have a lot of fun pairing different kinds of characters together.

Step 1: Use basic shapes to build up the two figures (male and female) with a soft pencil. To make him look like he's actually holding her, draw the hero first, then construct her figure so it looks as if he's supporting her. Note that the hero is drawn in blue and the girl is in red for illustrative purposes only.

Step 2: Using a slightly harder pencil, in this case an HB, start to flesh out the characters, giving the superhero stocky legs and a wide girth for exaggeration. He's a pretty large guy, but add a goofy grin and he is smitten like a little kid with a kitten. The woman is tiny by comparison, but keep her proportions more realistic. Now it's time to scan the image into Photoshop at 300 dpi.

Step 3: In Photoshop set the brush to dark grey using the Colour Picker, to better match the pencil lines and the brush option to Multiply. This will look more natural than flat digital painting over a real drawing. Use a 5 px round brush to clean up the entire image, focusing on hands and faces, then move into details like clothing seams and folds.

Step 4: Add a new layer set to Multiply. Lay down flat colours that cover large sections. It's easier to block in simple flat colours first before shading or adding highlights. Use the Polygonal Lasso tool to select large areas and the Paint Bucket to fill in the colour, then switch to a smaller brush (3 px or 5 px Round) to work in the smaller areas. For this example, the girl has khaki-coloured trousers instead of jeans to keep her from looking too much like a teenager; her bright colour scheme helps set her off against his red suit.

Step 5: Use the Eyedropper tool to select the red of the hero's suit and then go to the Colour Picker. Choose a red a few shades darker and then a few shades lighter to accent his suit. Too many colours and he'll look like a

clown, so stick just with reds. Selecting the lighter red, work in his facemask, boots and the details on the front of his shirt. Work in some of the shadowy areas using the darker red and a 9 px Soft Brush. Select the Burn tool set to 30% and notice the effect it has when you touch the cursor to the coloured areas of the drawing – it instantly darkens that area, creating a great shadow effect.

Step 6: Selecting an orange colour for highlights, set the brush option from Normal to Colour Dodge and add in some highlights. The right highlights on the suit will give a sense of texture – if they are strong enough, the suit will seem plastic; if they are dull, it will seem like soft fabric. You'll have to decide what kind of material your hero wears.

Chapter 6
Costumes

COMIC BOOK HEROES BEGAN IN THE PULP MAGAZINES – SO IT'S NATURAL THAT THEY ARE A DIVERSE GROUP. THEIR ROOTS LIE IN THE CIRCUS, THEREFORE A LOT OF THEIR COSTUMES REFLECT THE SKINTIGHT, BRIGHTLY COLOURED SUITS OF ACROBATS AND CIRCUS STRONGMEN.

COSTUME BASICS

Probably the most iconic of superhero costumes is that of the natural do-gooder. The kind of hero who saves a bus-load of people before they go over the edge of a cliff and then races back to save a kitten stranded on a tree branch. They wouldn't wear a mask – this is a hero kids look up to.

Dressing the superhero in warm colours (red, yellow, orange) gives him a sunny disposition that fits his character.

His counterpart in the female world of heroes might be dressed in a similar manner, but you can always play with colour schemes and see what else you can come up with.

At the opposite end of the superhero spectrum is the antihero – a darker and more sinister figure who isn't always clearly on the side of the good guys. These characters are the bad boys and girls of the superhero world and their costumes usually feature a mask and gloves to hide their identity.

The female version shows some of the details that make the antihero a bit more 'real' – the seams on her suit and the pads on her elbows and knees.

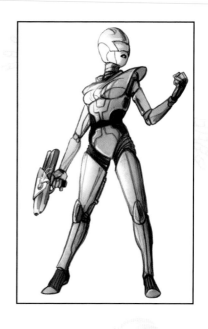

Having her hair jut out of the back of her cowl is probably not very practical, but it sure looks cool.

Note, by leaving the eyes white on this character's mask we give it an air of mystery.

Increasingly popular in the past few years, especially since the release of the Iron Man movies, is the technological superhero. Above we've got a no-holds-barred armoured crime fighter who still manages to maintain her femininity thanks to some finely shaped armour pieces.

Masks

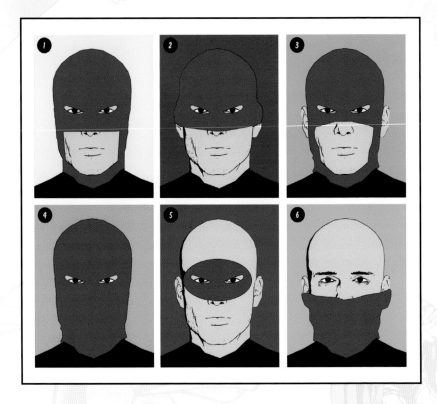

There are many mask options when you are designing the hero's costume –
the mask is one of the most important elements of the character. Let's take a
really simple design look at different kinds of masks.

Most mask styles are based on just a few concepts, as demonstrated here.

1 The three-quarter cowl. Covers most of the head but keeps the mouth area open.

2 The half-mask. Usually a mask like this ties at the back. Zorro swashbuckled in this design.

3 The three-quarter cowl with alterations. More of the nose is visible and for some reason the character's ears are visible. A variation on this mask has the top open so the hair shows through.

4 The full-face mask. In reality this probably provides the best disguise, since the entire face is hidden.

5 The domino mask. Provides the least identity protection.

6 An odd choice – kind of a scarf covering the lower-face. The Shadow and The Vigilante (original version) went with this one.

In the good old days fans weren't all that picky about what the mask was made out of. Today's fans are much more involved in questions when it comes to character details – is the mask cloth or leather? Does it have a built in helmet? A built in mobile phone? These and other questions may have to be answered by you – the hero's creator.

Accessories

An accessory can become a prop or part of a superhero's look – from belts and capes, to weapons and even the car he or she rides in, don't overlook these additions.

Belts

If you give a hero a belt like the one below it can look a little plain. When designing a belt you want to make sure it seems like it would work – even if it's just a fantasy-style belt.

Above: Wrestlers and boxers have long had decorative belts to display their championship status.

Right: Look at the way the buckle works – the holes in the belt adjust the size and keep it in place.

Use references to create more realistic designs.

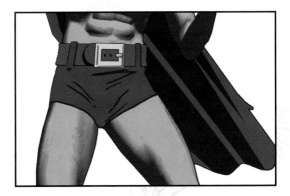

Superheroes don't have pockets. Using today's fashion, you could give the character a satchel.

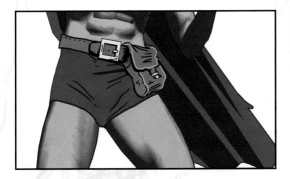

A more popular choice might be a belt with pouches, like you might find in military issue.

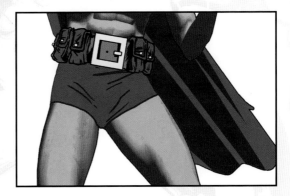

Hats

The Shadow was known for his slouch hat.

The Green Hornet opted for a more traditional fedora.

Hats are usually combined with a mask to aid in the disguise.

Capes

Capes come in a wide variety of shapes and sizes.

Above: The traditional medium-length cape. Note how it moves with the body, emphasising the motion of the figure.

Above: This style is longer and more draped – usually cascading out in an unrealistic dimension to show the mysterious nature of its wearer.

Above: This shorter version is usually reserved for the sidekick or female superheroes.

The wide-collar style is good for the avenger-type crusader.

The snap-buckle style of cape is simple and effective.

A hood can be added, which creates an interesting style.

Capes aren't always practical in fighting crime, but they were originally used as a method to demonstrate motion and movement of super characters and of course they owe a lot to their circus performer inspiration who often wore one as they came out into the centre ring.

The final cape is attached to the costume at the shoulders.

Boots

Adding details to the boots, even if they are minor ones, goes a long way towards improving the illustration.

Even something we might consider a 'generic' boot has style. Look at the tapered ankle and the stitching in this example (1). With superheroes the traditional manner of boot is usually tall, above mid-calf in length and often tapered to a point for some reason (4). Some boots mimic the look of the pirate boot with their flap at the top (2). Boots can be made up from combinations of other styles too – something short and sporty works for a dare-devilish type of urban adventurer (3).

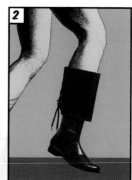

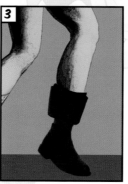

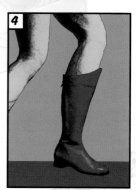

Many female heroes wear boots that look great but are completely impractical – especially when they are high-heeled. Choosing a more practical boot will give your character a more modern feel.

Drawing capes

A big mistake a lot of artists make when they draw superheroes with long, draping capes is that they just draw the cape itself and not the figure. Just because the character is wearing a cape does not mean you never have to draw the body again.

Step 1: It's important still to draw the whole figure so that you can accurately drape the cloth around it.

Step 2: Start at the point where the cape is clasped, in this case under his neck and then draw the lines flowing out towards and over the arms.

Step 3: The cape will then hang down from the point where it crosses over each arm. Draw this as a single shape as far as possible.

Step 4: To give the cape the appearance of volume, create another shape that comes off the outer edge of the cape that you've just drawn. This also gives the impression that it has folds.

Step 5: Finally, tweak the cape's edge with a few more shapes and folds, adding yet more volume.

From the back

If you wanted to draw the same type of cape from behind you'd first draw the figure from the opposite angle.

Then drop in the forms of the cape with an emphasis on the wrinkles and 'bunching up' that would be created at the back of the neck. Note that the edge of the cape on the right side is given volume by using the same technique for building up the shapes as before.

Muscled hero costume

Let's bring back our muscled figure from Chapter 3 (see page 110).

Step 1: Scan the drawing into Photoshop at 300 dpi, then adjust it by going to Image>Adjustment>Brightness/Contrast – use the slider bar to darken the lines.

Step 2: Use a 9 px round brush to draw a cape behind him.

Step 3: Add a layer set to Multiply and give the character some colour. Here blues, reds and yellows are used. He's also got red hair – which is unusual for a superhero – most of them have black hair, with blonde coming in a distant second, but red is almost unheard of.

Step 4: Add a new layer called 'Shadow', set to Multiply. Use the Magic Wand tool to select the white area around the figure (make sure you get the area under his right arm too). Then go to Select>Inverse and fill this area with grey using the Paint Bucket tool. The figure will now be in shadow.

Step 5: Use the Polygonal Lasso to cut away pieces of the shadow – in this case you want the light to be shining right on the hero, so the front of the character will be free of shadow.

Step 6: Zoom in and work on the details of the face and other areas of the character. Use a 5 px hard round brush to add black outlines and tighten up the drawing. Add eyes by first painting in the white, then a dot of blue with a smaller dot of black and an even smaller dot of white.

Step 7: You need some kind of background, but keep it simple. Go to Layer>Flatten image and then Layer>Duplicate layer – click on the bottom layer and add a layer. Use the Paint Bucket to fill this with white and then go to the top layer and select the white around the figure with the Polygonal Lasso tool. Hit delete and now, when you look at the Layers palette, you'll see that the figure is 'floating' in the middle of the illustration. This will allow you to work behind the figure easily.

Step 8: Now go to the white layer in the middle of the Layers palette – use the Elliptical Marquee tool to create a series of circles and a ground line using teal and black. Add a new layer (still behind the floating character layer) and use the Polygonal Lasso tool to create two searchlight beams and fill them with yellow.

Step 9: Because the searchlight beams are on a layer above the green background, you can go to Opacity in the Layers palette and bring it down to about 80%, so that some of the green will show through. Flatten the whole image by going to Layer>Flatten Image and you're done.

Lean, muscled hero costume

Let's finish up this one from Chapter 3 (see page 112).

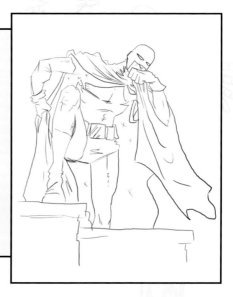

Step 1: Starting where you left off and using all of the accessory and costume details discussed earlier in the chapter, finish off the illustration using a fine tip mechanical pencil. Here we've gone with the short gloves, three-quarter cowl and pouch-style belt for his uniform.

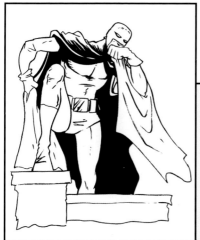

Step 2: Using a No. 2 round brush and black ink work in the details on top of the pencil drawing – once it has completely dried, erase the pencil lines. Keep the line work simple.

Step 3: To add a bit of mystery to the character, throw a bit more shadow on the piece – the front of the cowl and the area that would fall in shadow behind his cape.

Step 4: Scan the image into Photoshop at 300 dpi. Add a layer set to Multiply and work in the colours. Keep the colour scheme dark.

Step 5: Now concentrate on the details of the brick building he's standing on. Using a No. 3 brush and some dark red, start to draw in the shapes of the bricks. Then fill in those shapes with a mixture of different shades of reds and browns.

Step 6: Keep the bricks 'organic' – keep them from looking too neat and clean. Give them jagged edges.

Step 7: The space between the bricks looks a bit too white and clean, so take a few shades of grey and use a No. 59 brush to tap in some shading – just a bit here and there.

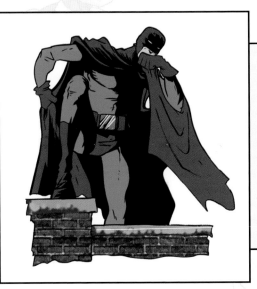

Step 8: Repeat the same process for the other set of bricks and then work in a little bit of 'weathering' for the grey stone area above those bricks, using the same method.

Step 9: Using the Paint Bucket tool, fill in the remaining white area around the figure with black. Add a layer above the Figure layer and use the Polygonal Lasso tool to create shadows on top of the brick building – giving the character a moody feel.

Skinny hero costume

This continues where you left off in Chapter 3 (see page 114).

Step 1: Take the layout drawing and work in some details in pencil – again, use the ideas covered in the accessories section of this chapter.

Step 2: Try giving him scalloped bat wings instead of a cape. Make sure the line on his left waist up to his chest muscle shows this. To make the scallops, start at the armpit and work down a 'vein' to each point.

Step 3: Scan the figure into Photoshop at 300 dpi and work out a colour scheme that works for his design using Multiply layers.

Exaggerated hero costume

This continues where you left off in Chapter 3 (see page 116).

Step 1: First, choose the costume elements. He could use a bit more shadow on the figure, too, so work on that. Go over the pencil lines with ink and a No. 2 round brush and then let it dry completely. Once it's dry, erase the pencil lines with a soft white eraser.

Step 2: Scan the drawing into Photoshop at 300 dpi and work in the colour scheme. Draw a lightning-bolt logo on the front of his costume using the Polygonal Lasso tool.

Step 3: Add a layer and draw a belt using the Polygonal Lasso tool. Fill it with an orange colour when you're happy with it.

Step 4: Go to Layer>Layer style>Stroke.

Step 5: This new box will pop up – it automatically defaults to size 3; bring it up to size 6 and click OK.

Step 6: This will put a black outline around the belt and make it look finished.

WEAPONS

t's a fact of the superhero genre that there is often weaponry in use. Whether it's the good guy or the bad guy, you'll need to draw some weapons.

Cartoon gun

Any weapon can be drawn by simply breaking it down into basic shapes – in this first example you can see a cartoon-style gun.

Step 1: Using a soft coloured pencil, put together a pyramid (triangle) and three cylinders. These are the basic shapes of all guns.

Step 2: Tighten it up a bit. Understanding how a gun works is important in getting it to look right – a gun consists of a handle, a trigger, a muzzle and a firing pin.

Step 3: Use some black ink to outline the shapes and you'll have a gun any cartoon bad guy might like.

A more realistic gun

If you want a bit more realism and a bit less styling you'll need to look at some reference. Looking online can usually yield a picture of a hand gun.

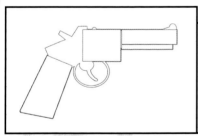

Step 1: The drawing is still made up of very basic shapes – a handle, trigger, firing pin, bullet chamber and muzzle.

Step 2: Tighten up the shapes with a pencil, adding details such as the safety switch, which sits right next to the firing pin and the aiming target on the end of the muzzle.

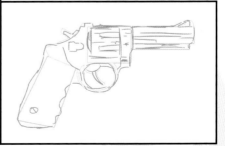

Step 3: Use a medium black marker to finish off the illustration. Making the handle all black is a good way to make it look finished. Use a ruler to do the straight lines and add a good amount of shadow to show form.

You can use these same methods to create any kind of weapon, man-made or alien – it's simply a matter of using simple shapes to build up the form and then using reference to work out the details.

Uzi submachine gun

This is a popular weapon because of its ability to fire a lot of bullets at once, despite its small size.

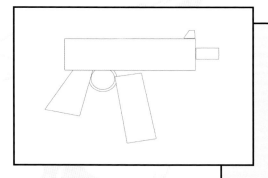

Step 1: Start out with almost the same shapes as for the revolver. Here there is the added magazine, which also works as a second handle to help control the gun when it's being fired.

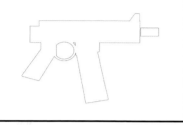

Step 2: Close off and tighten those shapes a bit more. This is the basic outline of the Uzi.

Step 3: Using reference, tighten up the drawing with a soft pencil. There are a lot of shapes and little details that make the design of the gun more interesting; you don't have to show them exactly, just indicate them.

Step 4: Finally, using a medium black marker and a ruler, fill in the black areas – keeping the light source up above means you'll have heavier shadows underneath to indicate that the gun has form and isn't just flat. Using stipple on the magazine gives it a metallic appearance.

CARS

You can draw any car – realistic, stylised or completely made up – if you just start by breaking it down into shapes and follow the rules of perspective (see page 52).

Step 1: Using a soft coloured pencil, put together a pyramid (triangle) and three cylinders. These are the basic shapes of all guns.

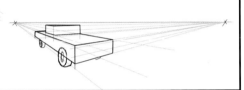

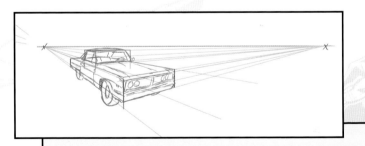

Step 2: Add in some interesting details to the car, using reference for the headlights and the interesting grille. The cab of the car tilts inwards and you can draw in a simple interior.

Step 3: Ink the lines of the car using a medium black marker. Don't worry too much about details. Keeping a few stray lines on the hood and the side edges of the car will hopefully give the impression of a high wax shine. Let the ink dry completely and erase the pencil lines.

Step 4: Add in some details, like a rearview mirror, an antenna and a side view mirror. For the tyres and the front licence plate take a little bit of white acrylic paint and a small No. 1 or No. 2 brush – it'll also work to put some more shine on the side of the car if you end up going too dark. Take the No. 2 brush and some black ink and make some loose and fat stippling on the car's headlights to give them some texture.

Chapter 7
Super environments

YOU'VE GOT TO HAVE A PLACE FOR THE HEROES AND VILLAINS TO HANG OUT, RIGHT? THERE'S A RICH HISTORY OF COMICS FEATURING IMAGINATIVE SECRET HEADQUARTERS AND SINISTER HIDDEN LAIRS. THE JAMES BOND VILLAINS HAVE OFTEN BEEN REFERRED TO AS COMIC BOOKISH, DUE MOSTLY TO THEIR ELABORATE HEADQUARTERS.

CHARACTER SETTINGS

Environments are more than just interesting backgrounds; they give the characters settings and aid in the stories you are trying to tell. Otherworldly universes, underground lairs, mad labs or far-off castle dungeons present great possible backdrops for the superhero.

Wonderman often battled crazed villains like Dr Voodoo and Lilith on far-off futuristic worlds.

Above: Wonderman: opening story page from Wonder Comics.

Wonderman's creators, who worked out of the Will Eisner Studios in the 1940s, gave him exotic locales in which to have his adventures. Flying cars, gravity-defying bridges and a snowy landscape add up to this amazing city of ice.

Above: Wonderman arrives at the Ice City.

Dick Devens existed in a world filled with super aircraft and military advancements that were seen nowhere else.

Left: Dick Devens oversees the loading of one of the government's top-secret planes, so big and powerful it needs both wings and rotor blades.

Devens often got himself into a jam – even with limited details we can see the dark and murky shadows, steel walls and world-conquering machinery of the dreaded Octopus Men. The use of heavy shadows and arched doorways give the setting an 'out-of-the ordinary' feel that suits the bizarre villains.

Captain Flash often battled super-criminals who built entire cities underground. The architecture and bridges show us that this is a city of the future.

Meanwhile Samson faced the incredibly twisted world of Thorga, whose devilish laboratory featured a wide variety of elaborate test tubes, electrical devices and even a 'high frequency thought transmitter' in wide-screen.

Giving the villains an impressive fortress from which to stage their evil attempts at world domination gave them a tremendous advantage.

Right: Doc Samson in the bizarre world of Thorga.

Mastermind underground HQ

The guide to perspective will help you to follow these simple steps to achieving a sinister underground headquarters for the villains (see page 52).

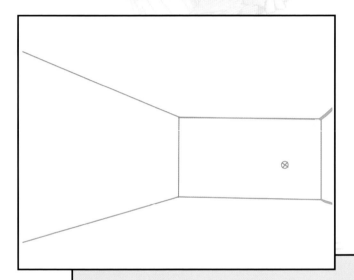

Step 1: The best way to start creating an elaborate environment is to begin very simply, with a square room. In Photoshop, use the Line tool to construct a basic space. Choose a vanishing point – here shown by the X in the circle – and make sure all the tops and bottoms of the room's elements go to the centre of the X.

Step 2: Once you have the basic space laid out, it's easy to start building more stuff inside. Think about the villain. What are they doing in here? Is it a luxurious castle interior? Or a laboratory in an eighteenth-century dungeon? This will be an elaborate workspace for the villain to build big, evil things. They'll need trucks, large vents and powerful, scientific interfaces; maybe even a cool catwalk.

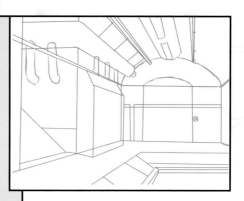

Step 3: Let's say this lair is controlled by an evil guy with lots of employees and they need this place to construct their rocket. The tiny size of the builders makes the space feel huge. It's important to establish the scale of the environment. Putting the rocket-builders in a recessed floor gives more depth to the room. And why not throw in a tank with an octopus, over on the left? The circle breaks up all of the rectangular elements and it's just plain fun.

Step 4: When the lair's ready for the details, print it out and use it like a blueprint. Using a lightbox, start drawing the finished drawing on a new piece of paper. Use a ruler to make sure the perspective is correct. Remember to keep in mind the texture of things – are they sleek, metallic surfaces or rock walls? Put in all of the little things that make a room interesting – buttons, switches, signs, props, wires; anything to make it look 'lived in'.

Step 5: Finish the drawing with some simple pencil shading. Keep in mind where the light sources are. For this construction site, they'll need bright florescent lights up top and maybe the loading docks on the left are lit for the trucks.

Step 6: Scan the finished drawing into Photoshop. Create a new layer and change it from Normal to Multiply. Choose a colour that will be on the majority of surfaces – in this

case, a greyish teal, for an industrial feel. Reinforce the lighting choices and choose a lighter version of that same colour for the rest. Start to pull out important elements, like the rocket, for example, using a bright yellow.

Step 7: Finish colouring, keeping with a colour scheme that works for the environment. For this evil lair, the more saturated the colours are, the more they make it feel like it belongs to a goofy, James Bond-style villain. If the colours are less vibrant, the overall feeling will be more serious. It's up to you.

Superhero flat

A superhero's flat, on the other hand, might feature some secret sliding gadgets and a spectacular view.

The important thing is to think creatively, using your imagination. An issue of *Architectural Digest* is great to have handy so you can get ideas for furnishing such a place, like the fur carpet or the nice rubber plants used here.

Think of yourself like a set designer for a movie when you're trying to depict environments and again, using your imagination is important. In this case, let's set a very modern building up on top of a mountain that overlooks a city in the distance.

Environments also depict the situation the superhero is in and clue the viewer in on what they're all about. Take a look at this one (left).

It's clear from this illustration of the superhero KO that he protects a city or is an urban adventurer.

Captain Flash is a superhero at the opposite end of the spectrum, fighting bizarre aliens in outer space, protecting not just one city – but the whole world.

Google SketchUp

One of the newest and greatest new programs is Google SketchUp, an amazing – and free – program that allows you to depict buildings, interiors and exteriors, bridges and all manner of manmade constructions. It is available to download at sketchup.google.com.

More than just allowing you to virtually build something – the program allows you to zoom in and around the object and position the 'camera' any way you like to capture unique shots using great background images.

Glossary

Bristol paper: A special double-surfaced heavy weight paper used for technical drawing and illustration.

Complementary colours: Opposite colours that intensify each other when used together.

Composition: The placement or arrangement of visual elements or ingredients in a work of art, as distinct from the subject of a work.

Cubism: Using a blocky, powerful style, cubism abandons single-point perspective and presents subjects from different viewpoints simultaneously.

Expressionism: A style of drawing used to express emotions through the use of strong, distorted lines and vivid colours, rather than attempting to capture a likeness or reality.

Half-tone: This is the transitional area from the shade into the light. The more gradual the turn of the form, the more half-tone there is. An object with a sharp edge in light and shade – like a box – will have little or no half-tone.

Hatching: The use of fine lines, often rapidly drawn, running parallel to each other, sometimes varying the spacing or lineweight. Types of hatching include cross-hatching, free-hatching and patch-hatching.

Mangaka: Japanese cartoon artists.

Minimalism: Artists, such as Alex Toth and Chris Ware, work with a simple style of line, retaining an element of realism while keeping a clean look by putting down as few lines as possible.

Perspective: Systems of representation in drawing and painting that create an impression of depth, solidity and special recession on a flat surface.

Realism: A style of drawing that is less exaggerated than cubism, focussing instead on reality and maintaining more realistic proportions.

Stippling: A drawing technique where you apply tone and texture in small dots. The dots are of a single colour so the denser the dots, the darker the apparent shade. This is not the same as pointillism, which uses dots of different colours.

Tone: The enhancing effect of adding grey to black and white artwork. Used to emphasise form, mood and shadow.

Vanishing point: In linear perspective, the point on the horizon at which receding parallel lines meet.

Wacom: A digital tablet used by artists for drawing on.

Index

Credits

All other images are the copyright of Quintet Publishing Ltd. While every effort has been made to credit contributors, Quintet Publishing would like to apologise if there have been any omissions or errors – and would be pleased to make the appropriate corrections for future editions of the book.

T = top, L = left, C = center, B = bottom, R = right, F = far

ILLUSTRATION CREDITS
Andy Fish
12, 13B, 14, 15, 30, 31L, 31R, 35T, 35B, 38, 39, 40, 41, 43T, 43B, 44, 45, 46, 47, 50, 51, 52, 54, 55, 56, 57, 58, 59, 60, 61, 62, 63, 64, 65, 67, 68, 69, 70, 71B, 72, 73, 88, 89, 95Bl, 95BR, 96, 97, 98, 99, 100, 104, 105, 106, 107, 108, 109, 110BL, 111, 112BR, 113, 115, 116, 117, 118, 119, 122, 123, 124, 125, 126, 127, 128, 129, 130, 131, 132, 136, 137, 138, 139, 148, 149, 150, 151, 152, 153, 154, 155, 156, 157, 158, 159, 160, 161, 165, 167, 168, 169, 170, 171, 172TL, 172TR, 173, 174, 175T, 175BL, 176R, 177, 178, 179, 182, 183, 184, 186TR, 187, 188, 189, 190, 191, 192, 193, 194, 195, 196, 197, 198, 199, 200, 201, 202, 203, 204, 205, 206, 207, 208, 209, 214, 215, 216, 217, 218
Veronica Fish
140, 141, 142, 143, 144, 145, 146, 147, 177, 178, 179
J.J. Hahrs & Veronica Fish
100R

IMAGE CREDITS
Apple.com
37
Dick Blick Art Supplies
32T, 32B, 33T, 33B, 34TL, 34TC, 34BR, 36T, 36CL, 36CR, 71T
JC Penney
186BR
UKW Wrestling
186L

Other
7, 11, 13TL, 18, 20TR, 22B, 27B © **Getty Images**; 8 © **Condé Nast Publishing**; 9 © **Beatty Bros Circus**; 91 © **Columbia Pictures**; 92B, 93T © **Osamu Tezuka**; 93BC, 93BR © **Naoki Urasawa.**